COLLECTOR'S ENCYCLOPEDIA OF

Lefton CHINA

BOOK II

Loretta De Lozier

COLLECTOR BOOKS

A Division of Schroeder Publishing Co., Inc.

Searching for a Publisher?

We are always looking for knowledgeable people considered to be experts within their fields. If you feel that there is a real need for a book on your collectible subject and have a large comprehensive collection, contact Collector Books.

Cover design: Beth Summers
Book design: Joyce Cherry

On the cover:
12" Provincial man and woman, carrying baskets of flowers.
#4141. $270.00 – 340.00 pair.

Contents

Introduction to Lefton Collecting...6

The National Society of Lefton Collectors...6

Getting Online..6

History of Lefton China...7

The Changing Market Place...8

Lefton Factories 9

Marks 10

Paper Labels of the Early Decades of Lefton China.................................12

Rare Items 13

Angels 17

Animals..22

Banks 28

Bedroom and Bathroom Accessories...30

Birds 34

Boxes 40

Candleholders..45

Christmas Items..48

Compotes...65

Cookie Jars and Canister Sets..68

Cups and Saucers...73

Decorative Items...80

Espresso Line..84

Figurines 86

Gingham Line...106

Jam, Instant Coffee, and Tea Jars 108

Kitchen and Table Accessories 111

Pitchers and Bowls...118

Planters...122

Plates 134

Salt and Pepper Shakers 138

Smoking Items..141

Snack Sets 148

Sugars and Creamers 151

Teapots and Coffee Pots 156

Tidbit Trays 162

Vases 164

Wall Plaques and Wall Pockets 173

Introduction to Lefton Collecting

Many of the Lefton items were produced in several sizes with different colors, designs, poses, and styles. Tableware also came in a variety of shades, shapes, and patterns.

Many Lefton items carry marks, identification numbers, and paper labels, although some were sold with only one of the three. Paper labels are often lost through washing or other wear. Resale value of pieces will be higher if all identifying marks are present, but until you become more familiar with the Lefton look of quality and appearance, you can be safe buying pieces with fired-on trademarks. You should be careful using paper labels as the only means of identification.

Item numbers may represent two or more different pieces. Therefore, when communicating with dealers and collectors, it becomes very important to give a clear description of the item you are discussing. This should include such details as texture of the finish and the piece's size, shape, and color. For dating purposes, it is essential that you describe the trademarks of the item.

The National Society of Lefton Collectors

The National Society of Lefton Collectors is a growing group. Through a quarterly newsletter, members share stories about their personal collections and advertise in search of missing pieces for their collections. In addition, members notify others of pieces they are willing to sell.

Excellent cooperation has been established with other clubs and societies also interested in Lefton items. These include collectors of cookie jars, salt and pepper shakers, tea and toast sets, chintz patterns, teapots and ashtrays. Although Lefton China stands alone as a collectible, its place with many other collectors is being learned through newsletter exchanges.

You are strongly encouraged to join the National Society of Lefton Collectors to develop a great line of communication with other Lefton collectors.

GETTING ONLINE

The Lefton collecting frenzy is widespread. From Washington to Florida and from Arizona to Maine, the word is out and the number of collectors is expanding daily. To help keep pace with the communication demands as we move into a new century, I am now on Internet and can be reached at LeftonLady@aol.com. Please check your members' directory for any changes to my electronic address. Look forward to hearing from you.

History of Lefton China

Any writer of history should make a sincere effort to be concise and accurate. Much of history occurs with little or no written documentation and revisiting the events that make history permits an author to add a little personal flavor, making history neither fact nor fiction. So, in the case of this historical record of Lefton China, I hope you will trust my information. I assure you, this is an honest account of the creation of a long-to-be-remembered china importing and marketing organization.

Lefton China is the brainchild of George Zoltan Lefton. Hungarian born and bred, he had a sense for business as American as Henry Ford's or John Rockefeller's. Mr. Lefton found gold along the streets of Chicago. It didn't come from the ground and wasn't smelted in a furnace, but was created through beautiful products cherished by thousands of people in both the present and the future.

Lefton's own written historical description begins simply:

In the mid-1930s George Zoltan Lefton, a native of Hungary, was earning a living by designing and manufacturing sportswear. As a hobby, he collected fine porcelain.

Seeking freedom and opportunity, Lefton set sail for America in 1939. He arrived in Chicago and his passion for collecting porcelain began to shape ideas for a new business. By early 1941, Lefton's desire for quality ceramics overpowered any feelings he might have had for fabric and fashion, so he created his own ceramics business.

At the conclusion of World War II, he saw the opportunities for reviving the Oriental skills in porcelain and importing them for the American consumer. It wasn't long before he found himself deeply planted in the industry, importing giftware from the Orient and being unofficially known as the "The China King." Today, the company is the leading producer of ceramic giftware and its products are found in gift shops around the world.

Though this little bit of rhetoric meets my criteria for expressing history, concise and accurate, it leaves out events that made Mr. Lefton's efforts unique in the porcelain industry.

Between the first and second paragraphs of that brief history occurred World War II, beginning on Sunday morning, December 7, 1941. When that historical event was known in Chicago, it was early Sunday afternoon. Mr. Lefton had a Japanese-American friend and business neighbor whom he valued as one of his own relatives. Upon hearing of the Japanese attack on Pearl Harbor, without any fanfare he proceeded to board up the unprotected glass front of his friend's business.

And not a minute too soon. Almost gang like, Chicago residents moved through the streets, identifying Japanese citizens, threatening bodily harm and destroying every Japanese-owned business they could reach until law and order was restored.

This same friend played an important role in Mr. Lefton's selection of Japan as his major manufacturing source for some common and extremely rare items we collect which carry the familiar Lefton paper label or fired-on mark.

Mr. Lefton continued to add Japanese and other Oriental manufacturers to his list of suppliers. Until very recently, the majority of the items he marketed originated from Japanese sources. With the Lefton Company's continuing pursuit of quality specifications for its suppliers, items marketed today, regardless of their origin, will be in demand long into the future.

The Changing Market Place

The majority of collectors purchase from the usual sources, antique dealers and antique malls, with a few purchases made at auctions or from private collectors. Therefore, this guide is basically directed at the price the dealer would ask. Many dealers are also collectors and vice versa, making pricing a formidable challenge.

Just how does a dealer decide an asking price? Price guides like this help. The dealer's own experience and comparable pricing add credence. The price the dealer paid for the item certainly dictates to some degree what he anticipates the resale value might be.

Limited editions or other factors that reduce the quantity of a certain item usually add to its value. I say usually because my opinion has been altered in developing values for Lefton China. My search of Lefton's historical records shows a number of items maintained on inventory card were often cancelled after a very limited number were marketed. This was not the result of purposely creating a limited edition; it was simply the result of difficulties which made it very costly for the factory to continue production or failure of the piece to meet design expectations.

I have had the opportunity to visit auctions, antique malls, antique dealers, and private collectors from coast to coast and from border to border and, strangely enough, I find prices to be relatively consistent. The latest pricing information seems to spread quickly across the nation. Fewer good buys are available as people cling to their Lefton collections.

As in all fine china collecting, condition is a principal factor in the price. Unfortunately, the very thing that makes so many pieces of Lefton extremely desirable is the same thing that often causes a diminishing price. Most of the hand applied floral patterns are extremely delicate. Lefton chose to design flowers and leaves naturally with points and fine lines rather than with smooth, rounded edges. Therefore, it is difficult, if not impossible, to find perfect specimens of Lefton in their bisque series. However, my prices reflect values of items that are as close to being perfect as you can locate. Damaged pieces should be reduced in value as the purchaser perceives; remember, however, that you may have a long wait to find that perfect piece.

As you know, neither pricing nor appraising is a pure science. My prices will surely be challenged by some as too high and others as too low. However, I think my system of pricing by comparables and desirability is reliable and consistently reflects the current and real market place value. Undoubtedly, Lefton remains a relative new-to-the-industry collectible and as demonstrated over the last two years, its pricing structure will continue to make rapid adjustments and corrections. The world continues to be in a frenzy over collecting and Lefton remains an ideal choice for even the most sophisticated collector. Lefton gives the opportunity to collect a wide variety of sets, series, themes, combinations, clusters, colors, and patterns, making it a collector's dream.

Lefton Factories

From the very beginning, the principal source of Lefton China was factories in Japan. In the mid 1970s, the circumstances changed with regard to sources in Japan that apparently caused Lefton to seek factories and suppliers from other Oriental locations. Taiwan, Malaysia, Sri Lanka, and China, among others, have been added as principal sources since their factory quality and performance met Lefton's strict requirements. You are also going to find Lefton pieces that bear references to having been made in England and Italy. However, the majority of items sold by Lefton included in this price guide and now found in the secondary market place were manufactured in Japan.

Though many different factories were used to satisfy the high volume marketing ability of Lefton, the same or a very similar procedure was employed to introduce each piece to its customers.

The creation of almost every item of Lefton China began with a simple marketing idea. This was communicated to a designer who translated that idea into a sketch sufficient for a sculptor to mold and shape it into a three dimensional model. Once that shape was approved, a trial mold was made from which a new prototype was produced. If the prototype was satisfactory, a reliable master mold was made that permitted the manufacture of many production molds, each of which was used to produce only 25 to 30 quality items.

The items of the production run were fired, decorations and painting were added, and the item was refired. A few of the more intricate items might require three or more firings to provide the desired finish. Delicate leaves and flower petals were hand shaped from clay with a tool similar to a carver's gouge, or may have been formed in a simple mold, shaped, and carefully attached by hand or with tweezers. An assembly line technique was employed by many factories; production rates of 5,000 to 50,000 or more per month were commonplace, depending on the capability of the factory and the strict specifications or the delicateness of the item.

The quality standards of Lefton were well known to all factories that produced their items. Lefton managed to maintain its high level of quality control over the years because it was a high-volume company and could choose from many factories. If production quality fell below standards, Lefton's managers would take the items back or authorize their destruction and replace them with acceptable ones.

As a new collector of Lefton, you may have to turn a piece upside down to know for sure that it is Lefton. Later, as your eye becomes sharper, you will be nearly certain of the outcome before you turn the item over. This is what I call the Lefton difference.

Not unlike other ceramic and porcelain importing and marketing companies. Lefton's beginning placed little emphasize on developing a system for dating their products. Fortunately, however, a system did emerge that helps the collector.

Rather than use a standard mark created by the Lefton Company, the style, color, and type of mark were often left up the manufacturer. The Lefton Company references, as we know them today, began just after World War II; from 1940 to 1946 there may have been Lefton China that Mr. Lefton purchased and sold, but little is known about the marks that were used. Universal Statues made products for Mr. Lefton to sell domestically but my research has not uncovered any type of identification that would help the collector. The items made between 1945 and 1953 were labeled "Made in Occupied Japan", as was required by law during General MacArthur's administration of post-war Japan.

Most Lefton items are identified by a fired-on trademark or a paper label on the bottom of the piece. Also some pieces, made in the 1950s and later years, had the year of copyright placed below the trademark, but usually any number found there is the item identification number. Certain registered and unregistered trademarks and logos of George Zoltan Lefton Company have been appropriately credited. If the number is preceded by letters, these will be the abbreviated factory identification. Trademarks are found in both single color and multi-color styles. A few of the factory identifications are shown below and some of the marks used are pictured on the following pages.

SL–Nippon Art China K.K.
SG–G.K. Shimizu Toen Seitosho
YX–Yada Toki K.K.
C–K.K. Seiy
RH–Bito
YS–Yamagata Seitosho
WK–Wako Toki K.K.
MM–Maruyama Toki K.K.
H–K.K. Hichihonmatsu Toen
MU–Chikusa Boeki K.K.
TWK–Tong Fang Art China Co., Ltd.
HK–K.K. Hakuho
NP–Maruei Toki K.K.
YD–G. K. Marua Shoten
JT–Takagi Seito K.K.

KF–Kobayashi
PY–Miyao Toki K.K.
KW–Kowa Toki K.K.
YK–Yamakumi Seito K.K.
CY–Chubu Yogyo K.K.
NE–Endo Toki K.K.
YU–Yamamoto Seito Y.K.
TWA–Yeong Fuh Co., Ltd.
EM–K.K. Kanesho
OK–K.K. Kodama Toki
SX–Y.K. Setou Shokai
MR–K.K. Maruri Shokai
HP–Honji Togyo K.K.
PF–Moritomo Toki G. K.

Though there are many identification numbers that bear the same factory identification letters, this guide has avoided the use of most factory prefaces and uses only the numbers that would have appeared in the original Lefton inventory records and catalogs. You may find that there was more than one factory producing the same item and more than one item bearing the same number. Confusing? Of course it is. This is the reason that it will take both the number and the description to match to be certain you are talking about the same piece.

To add a little more to your knowledge of the numbering system, you will find suffix letters that are reasonably easy to explain. "R" may mean "rose", "V" may mean "violet", "S" may mean "small", "L" may mean "large"; but then "R" can also mean "right" and "L" can mean "left". As an informed collector, many other clues for identification will present themselves.

1946 – 1950

1946 – 1950

1946 – 1950

1946

1946 – 1953

1946 – 1953

1948 – 1953

1953 – 1975

1950 – 1957

1949 – 1964   1955 – Present   1968 +   1971 +

Almost every Lefton collector has become familiar with the various fired-on marks appearing on a large percentage of pieces. They have also observed the many differences in the paper labels that were used in addition to or in place of the fired-on marks. This edition of the *Collector's Encyclopedia of Lefton China* covers items from 1940 through 1960, with some pieces from the 1970s and a very limited amount from the 1980s. Both this and the first edition have concentrated on items that were manufactured in Japan. As noted previously, factories in other countries have manufactured and are still manufacturing many items for Lefton.

Specific date ranges of paper labels have been found for items through months of research and study of old records and old catalogs. There have been other labels used to identify Lefton pieces, but these will represent the ones you will see most frequently. Pictured below are the most common paper labels with dates to help a collector more accurately date Lefton items.

Label Description	Photo	Approx. years used
Large crimson red w/gold or silver trim. *Lefton's* EXCLUSIVES JAPAN		1946 – 1953
Standard Lefton label, red w/gold trim; infrequently w/silver trim. *Lefton's* Reg. U.S. Pat. Off. EXCLUSIVES JAPAN		1953 – 1971
Standard Lefton label, red w/gold trim. *Lefton* Trademark EXCLUSIVES JAPAN		1960 – 1983
Standard Lefton label, red w/gold trim. *Lefton (w/R in circle over "on" of Lefton)* Trademark EXCLUSIVES JAPAN		1962 – 1990

Rare Items

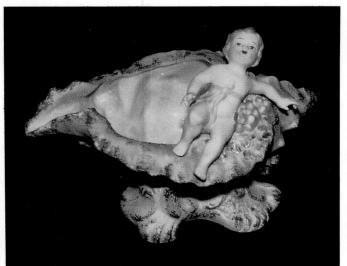

8½" Bowl, shell shaped with angel.
#959. $250.00 – 350.00.

7" Bowl, large shell shape with angel,
gray-green bisque with roses.
#926. $500.00 – 600.00.

Double vase with two angels playing instruments.
#591. $250.00 – 300.00.

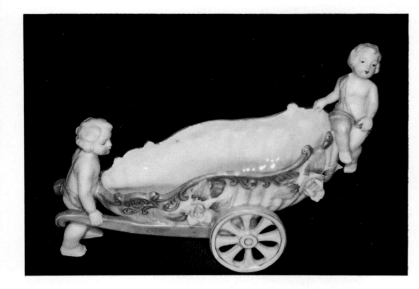

9¼" Cart with two angels in pastel green bisque with pink roses. #810. $250.00 – 300.00.

7"x5½" Candleholders with angels in pastel bisque with pink roses. #965. $125.00 – 150.00.

Cherub sitting on a limb in a cloud with stars and birds. #827. $100.00 – 125.00 each.

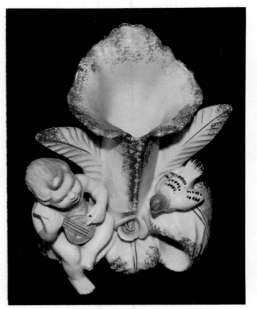

6½" Vase, bisque decorated with angel and bird.
#742. $150.00 – 175.00 each.

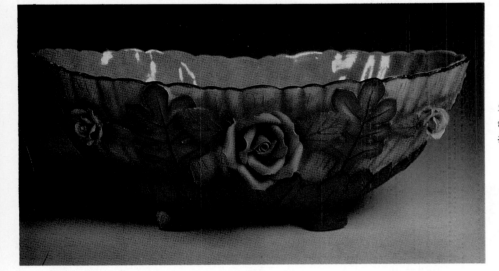

9¼" Bowl in pastel green bisque decorated
with pink roses, footed.
#773. $240.00 – 280.00.

6½" Well planter, pastel gray-green bisque finish
with colored birds.
#940. $65.00 – 75.00.

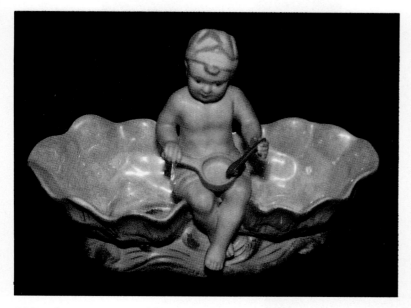

*8" Bowl, gray green pastel bisque finish with small boy on rim.
#942. $200.00 – 225.00.*

*5½" Leaf dish with sponge gold decoration and raised
pink flowers.
#962. $50.00 – 55.00.*

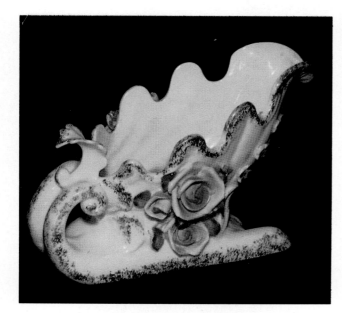

*7" Sled, white with sponge gold and pink roses.
#321. $105.00 – 125.00.*

*5" White china lyre vase, decorated in
sponge gold and raised roses.
#955. $65.00 – 75.00.*

Angels

4" Angel zodiac sign, Taurus.
#8650. $40.00 – 45.00.

3" Angel of the month, April.
#1987J. $45.00 – 55.00.

4½" Boy of the month, January.
#1952. $20.00 – 25.00.

5" Boy of the month, December.
#2300. $35.00 – 45.00.

5½" Boy of the month, April.
#556. $35.00 – 45.00.

4" Baby of the month, November.
#331. $22.00 – 28.00.

4½" Kewpie of the month, January.
#130. $35.00 – 40.00.

3¼" Angels sitting in flowers playing instruments.
#1699. $120.00 – 150.00 set of three.

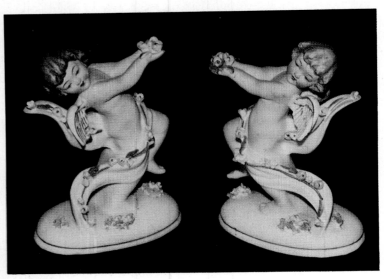

4½" Angels standing on base with applied flowers.
#8701. $130.00 – 160.00 pair.

4¾" Angel in bisque.
#2323. $35.00 – 45.00.

4" Angels, beautifully detailed glazed china with gold wings.
#808. $40.00 – 45.00 each.

5" Birthday girl with stone.
#6224. $25.00 – 35.00.

3½" Musical girls.
#149. $25.00 – 30.00 each.

4¾" Flower girls.
#110. $18.00 – 22.00 each.

Small musical girl plays "Happy Birthday."
#6985. $40.00 – 45.00.

4½" Birthday girl with stone.
#5146. $22.00 – 28.00.

Angel of the month.
#1987. $35.00 – 45.00 each.

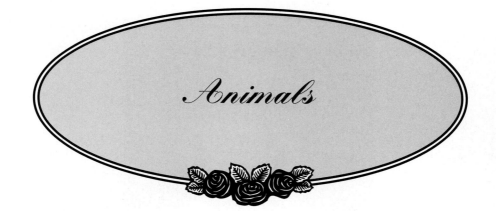

Animals

French Poodles with stones.
#80550. $45.00 – 55.00 set of three.

5" Poodles, white with lilacs.
#157. $40.00 – 45.00 each.

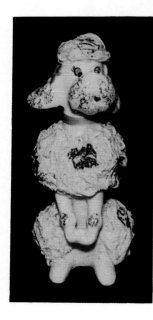

White poodle sitting up.
#064. $27.00 – 32.00.

5" Squirrel, bisque.
#4749. $35.00 – 38.00.

9" Wild hare.
#4493. $95.00 – 125.00.

5" Beaver, bisque.
#4747. $35.00 – 38.00.

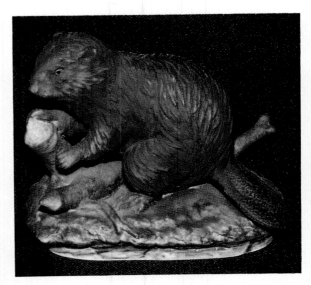

5½" Otter.
#132. $32.00 – 38.00.

5" Raccoon, bisque.
#4752. $42.00 – 48.00.

5½" Black bear, bisque.
#4912. $34.00 – 38.00.

5" Red fox, bisque.
#5058. $30.00 – 35.00.

9½" Fox and hare.
#352. $100.00 – 125.00.

10" Red fox, bisque.
#4757. $105.00 – 125.00.

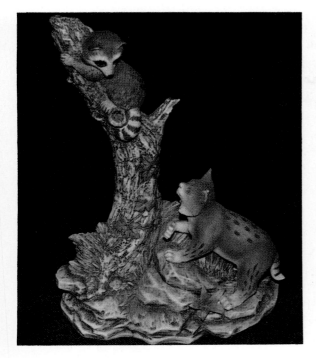

8¼" Bobcat and raccoon.
#351. $100.00 – 125.00.

7" Lion.
#7286. $13.00 – 18.00.

8½" Tiger, black, white, and gold.
#8743. $65.00 – 85.00.

8" Tiger, bisque.
#4950. $75.00 – 80.00.

Tiger.
#6761. $30.00 – 35.00.

6½" Leopard, bisque.
#6703. $32.00 – 38.00.

7" Cat and dog, luster with stones.
#871. $30.00 – 40.00 each.

5" Contemporary dog.
#9446. $40.00 – 45.00.

5" Dachshund with stones, matte.
#3213. $20.00 – 25.00.

3½" Persian cat, matte.
#1513. $10.00 – 15.00 each.

4½" Cat on pillow.
#2540. $15.00 – 20.00.

5⅝" Deer.
#521. $30.00 – 40.00.

4½" Fish.
#1072. $25.00 – 35.00.

Banks

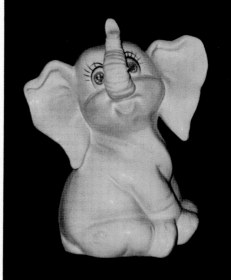

5½" Pig with roses, white.
#355. $30.00 – 40.00.

7" Pink elephant with stones.
#2429. $25.00 – 35.00.

5"x4" Pig with flowers.
#1992. $20.00 – 30.00.

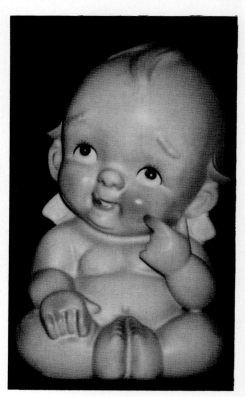

6¾" Kewpie.
#145. $65.00 – 75.00.

Turtle with glass eyes.
#3893. $11.00 – 14.00.

6" Lion wearing glasses.
#13384. $52.00 – 58.00.

4½" Mushroom shape with butterfly
and pixie. #879. $25.00 – 35.00.

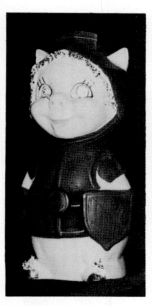

7" Pig with rhinestone eyes.
#90465. $42.00 – 52.00.

8" Girl, Lefton's Americana.
#069. $30.00 – 35.00.

Bedroom and Bathroom Accessories

7¼" Oval picture frame with cherubs.
#7221. $65.00 – 75.00.

Perfume set, two bottles and powder jar. French Rose.
#2649. $42.00 – 48.00.

4½" Pineapples, perfume set, two bottles and powder jar.
#9567. $90.00 – 120.00.

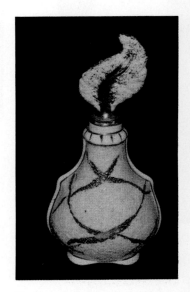

Perfume bottle, Eastern Elegance.
#128. $45.00 – 50.00.

*Perfume set, two bottles and pow-
der jar, Lilacs and Stones.
#233. $160.00 – 180.00.*

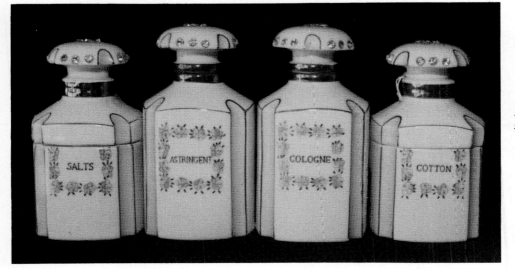

*Bathroom set with stones, 4 pieces.
#90045. $175.00 – 210.00.*

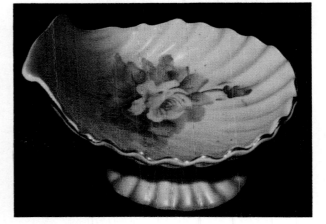

*Shell-shaped soap dish, footed.
#5066. $10.00 – 12.00.*

3½" Hand ringholder, pink bisque.
#90545. $22.00 – 28.00.

12½" Perfume tray, Tiffany Rose.
#982. $75.00 – 95.00.

5" Mermaid with bubble.
#60153. $30.00 – 35.00.

4½"x7" Sea horse with mermaid.
#528. $40.00 – 45.00.

6" Fish, black, white with sponge gold.
#60114. $33.00 – 38.00.

4" Ringholder with lipstick holder.
#442. $16.00 – 20.00.

3¾" Toothbrush holder, French Rose.
#2646. $15.00 – 20.00.

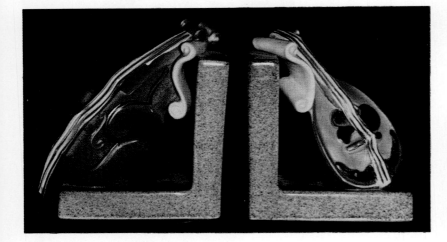

5½"x5" Bookends, violin and mandolin.
#018. $35.00 – 45.00.

3½" Pin cushions.
#542 & #543. $12.00 – 15.00 each.

5½" Double soap dish with cherub, Renaissance.
#3602. $15.00 – 30.00.

Birds

9½" Double bluebirds on a tree branch with wooden base, bisque. #655. $110.00 – 130.00.

6" Angel on leaves with bird, cardinal. #852. $60.00 – 65.00.

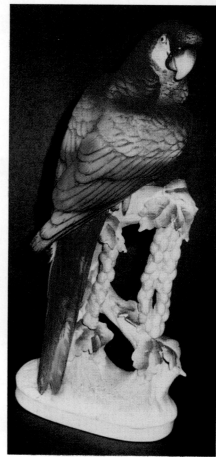

6½" Baby in bisque, goldfinch. #776. $35.00 – 45.00.

9¼" Macaw, brilliant colors #1055. $110.00 – 140.00.

11½" Duck.
#7555. $95.00 – 105.00.

5½" Heron.
#1532. $45.00 –55.00.

10¼" Woodpecker.
#5061. $95.00 – 100.00.

11" Eagle.
#802. $100.00 – 120.00.

5¾" California quail.
#760. $55.00 – 65.00 pair.

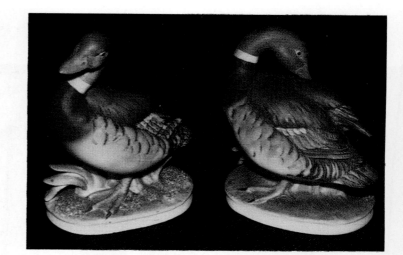

4" Mallard duck, bisque.
#2070. $38.00 – 48.00 pair.

3" Turkey.
#2255. $35.00 – 45.00.

4½" Turkey.
#6715. $22.00 – 27.00.

9" Quetzal.
#1054. $130.00 – 180.00.

7½" Waxwing on nest.
#3738. $62.00 – 68.00.

5½" Parakeet.
#465. $45.00 – 55.00.

8½" Toucan.
#1056. $125.00 – 155.00.

10" Long-tail rooster.
#1057. $125.00 – 145.00.

5¼" Bobwhite.
#300. $36.00 – 40.00.

7½" Owl and waxwing on wood base.
#8018. $200.00 – 250.00.

4½" Chickadee.
#6609. $20.00 – 25.00.

9" Golden pheasant with open wings.
#211. $195.00 – 225.00.

12" Pheasant with closed wings.
#210. $200.00 – 250.00.

7½" Pheasants.
#769. $95.00 – 110.00 pair

5" Cardinal.
#395. $22.00 – 27.00.

Owl.
#866. $23.00 – 28.00.

8¼" Goldfinch.
#5158. $52.00 – 60.00.

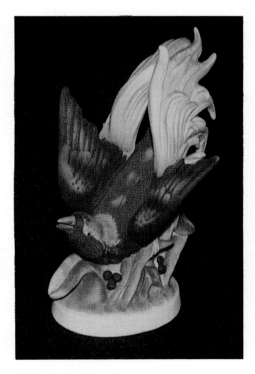

6¾" Bird of paradise.
#140. $75.00 – 85.00.

5" Ruffled grouse.
#2668. $35.00 – 45.00.

Boxes

White bisque with butterfly on lid.
#2771. $18.00 – 22.00.

4½" Egg-shaped candy with flowers
and bow on lid.
#4742. $17.00 – 23.00.

5" Hinged, egg-shaped, Spring Bouquet.
#335. $40.00 – 45.00.

4" Powder with rhinestones and flowers.
#90041. $45.00 – 55.00.

2¾" Pin, bisque floral bouquet.
#3780. $12.00 – 18.00.

4" Hinged boxes, Spring Bouquet.
#8134. $40.00 – 50.00 each.

6½" Candy, red with cherub on lid.
#2210. $35.00 – 40.00.

5¾" Candy, Valentine girl.
#7172. $22.00 – 28.00.

6¼" Musical hinged box, plays "Anniversary Waltz", Tiffany
Rose. #979. $50.00 – 60.00.

3" Covered and hinged, Antique Ivory Bisque.
#455. $12.00 – 15.00.

3¼" Powder, bone china.
#550. $18.00 – 21.00 each.

6¼" Candy, legged, Gold Leaf.
#3549. $40.00 – 45.00.

4½" Candy, 25th anniversary.
#2604. $18.00 – 23.00.

6½" Candy, Gold Laurel.
#2528. $24.00 – 28.00.

6½" x 7" Candy, Della Robbia.
#2089. $32.00 – 36.00.

6¼" Green Heritage.
#6131. $85.00 – 95.00.

7½"x4¼" Candy with handle and rose.
#365. $35.00 – 40.00.

4" Candy, red heart with angel on lid.
#2818. $10.00 – 12.00.

3½" Pink box with owl decoration.
#5090. $10.00 – 15.00.

3½" Open egg with chick and flowers, bisque.
#5549. $12.00 – 15.00.

5¼" Candy egg.
#548. $13.00 – 16.00.

Candleholders

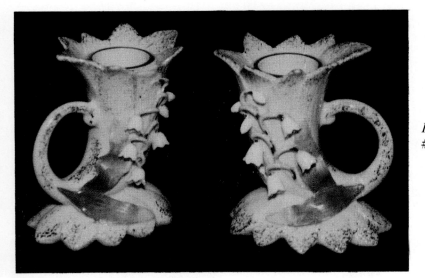

Pink china trimmed with sponge gold and Lily of the Valley.
#285. $48.00 – 58.00 pair.

4¾" white trimmed with sponge gold and roses.
#208. $45.00 – 55.00 pair.

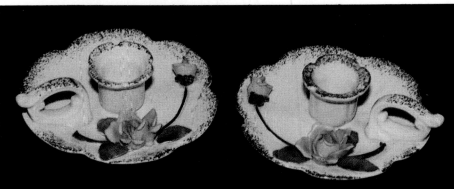

4" Pink china trimmed with sponge gold and yellow roses.
#907. $95.00 – 105.00 pair.

3½" Roses in pink, bisque.
#1848. $40.00 – 50.00 pair.

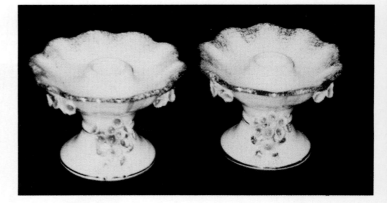

3" cherubs, Whiteware or Renaissance.
#3564. $12.00 – 18.00 pair.

3" Forget-Me-Not flowers.
#9827. $95.00 – 105.00 pair.

Pink with Forget-Me-Not flowers.
#771. $52.00 – 62.00 pair.

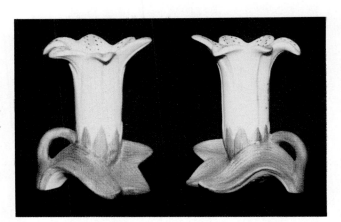

3¾" Lily.
#2499. $25.00 – 30.00 pair.

5½" Country Squire.
#1613. $23.00 – 28.00 pair.

6" Rustic Daisy.
#5408. $12.00 – 14.00.

Animal, 3¾" dog.
#7696. $8.00 – 12.00.

Candleholders, 4" little boy dressed in Santa suit.
#3051. $20.00 – 25.00 pair.

Candleclimber, 2" Santakin.
#4029. $5.00 – 10.00.

Candleholder, 4" angel votive.
#5286. $7.00 – 10.00.

Candleholder, 3½" Christmas girl.
_#6854. $8.00 – 12.00._

Figurine, 4½" Santa helper.
_#1734. $22.00 – 28.00._

3¼" Angel.
_#1419. $15.00 – 20.00._

Four little angels on candy cane.
_#626. $60.00 – 70.00._

Figurine, 4¼" Santas playing instruments.
#4482. $20.00 – 25.00 each.

Figurine, 4" Christmas girl.
#6604. $8.00 – 12.00.

Mug, 8" girl wearing Santa hat.
#3545. $8.00 – 12.00.

Figurine, 4½" Santa with angels.
#6112. $15.00 – 20.00.

Angel, small girl playing musical instrument.
#1259. $25.00 – 30.00.

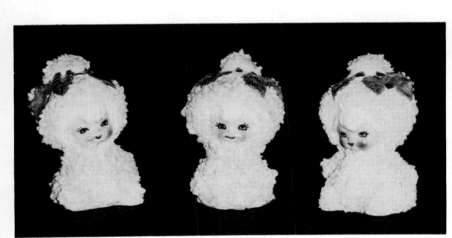

Figurine, 3" snow babies.
#4405. $35.00 – 45.00 set of three.

Figurine, 4½" Little Miss Mistletoe.
#102. $35.00 – 45.00.

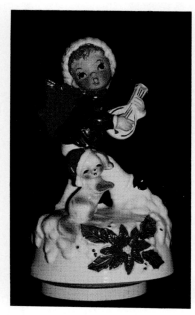

Box, 7"x6" candy Christmas sleigh.
#770. $60.00 – 80.00.

Box, 6½" figural, musical.
#7066. $40.00 – 50.00.

Bell, 4½" house with Santa.
#1336. $20.00 – 25.00.

Bell, 3¼" Santa.
#90400. $20.00 – 25.00.

Bell, Christmas girl.
#8250. $30.00 – 40.00.

Bell, 3½" angels spelling Noel.
#90283. $50.00 – 60.00 set.

Bell, Christmas snowball.
#019. $22.00 – 28.00.

Plate, 8" Christmas tree.
#1096. $28.00 – 32.00.

Decanter, 7¾" Santa.
#1383. $25.00 – 35.00.

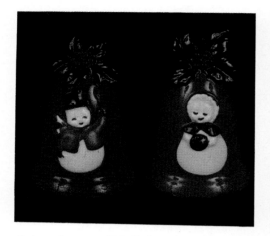

Salt and pepper, 3" bell-shaped.
#4281. $12.00 – 16.00.

4½" Poinsettia candle holders.
#8024. $25.00 – 45.00 pair.

Salt and pepper, Christmas tree with toothpick holder.
#054/96. $50.00 – 60.00.

Salt and pepper, Mr. and Mrs. Claus.
#071. $22.00 – 26.00.

Salt and pepper, Mr. and Mrs. Claus in sleigh.
_#314. $28.00 – 32.00._

Salt and pepper, 4" Santas.
_#3764. $15.00 – 20.00._

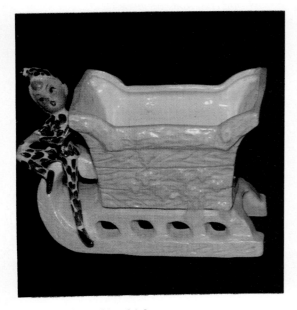

Planter, elf on white sleigh.
_#313. $18.00 – 22.00._

Christmas figurines, with violin or lantern, 4¾".
#072. $27.00 – 35.00 each.

Planter, 8" Santa with bag.
#3656. $23.00 – 27.00.

Planter, 8" girl with muff and hat, green.
#051. $40.00 – 45.00.

Shelf sitters, 5½" Mr. and Mrs. Claus.
#1996. $45.00 – 55.00.

Planter, 4½" Santa boot.
#1475. $18.00 – 22.00.

Planter, 4½" Christmas boot.
#2306. $22.00 – 28.00.

Pitcher and bowl, 3¾" Holiday Holly.
#7940. $22.00 – 28.00.

Box, 5½" candy, bisque Poinsettia.
#8026. $23.00 – 33.00.

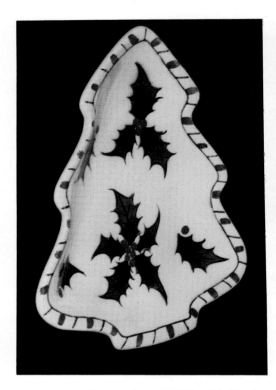

Bell, 9" White Christmas.
#2062. $10.00 – 15.00.

Bell, 3½" White Holly.
#6053. $8.00 – 10.00.

Dish, 8" x 7¼" tree-shaped Holly with Touches
of Candy Cane Red.
#1294. $40.00 – 45.00.

Bowl, 5" sleigh, White Holly.
#6048. $10.00 – 15.00.

Pitcher and bowl, 5" pitcher and 5½" bowl,
White Holly.
#6075. $19.00 – 23.00.

Candleholder w/candleclimbers, Green Holly.
#1360. $35.00 – 45.00 4-piece set.

Tray, two-tier tidbit, Green Holly.
#1364. $65.00 – 75.00.

Box, 8½" musical hors d'oeuvre, Green Holly.
#1365. $60.00 – 70.00.

Lamp, 5¾" kerosene, Green Holly.
#4863. $45.00 – 55.00.

Bowl, 5½" with handle, Green Holly.
#5175. $20.00 – 25.00.

Pitcher and bowl, 4" pitcher and 5½" bowl, Green Holly.
#5174. $15.00 – 20.00.

Candleholders, Green Holly.
#717. $25.00 – 30.00 pair.

Dish, single leaf-shaped, Green Holly.
#1347. $30.00 – 35.00.

Box, covered candy, Green Holly.
#1361. $25.00 – 30.00.

Salt and pepper, Green Holly.
#1353. $22.00 – 28.00.

Bell, 3½" Green Holly.
#787. $13.00 – 18.00.

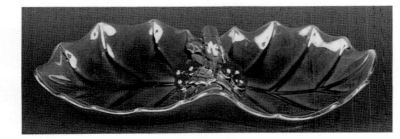

Dish, two compartment, Green Holly.
#1349. $22.00 – 28.00.

Sugar and creamer, Green Holly.
#1355. $45.00 – 55.00.

Teapot, 6 cup, Green Holly.
#1357. $75.00 – 85.00.

Bowl, 8" sleigh, Green Holly.
#1346. $45.00 – 55.00.

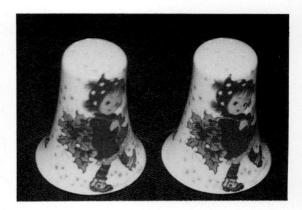

Salt and pepper, 2½" Christy.
#441. $18.00 – 22.00.

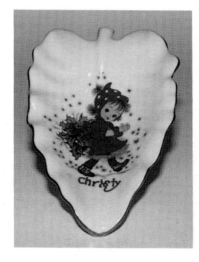

Dish, 6¾" Christy.
#443. $15.00 – 20.00.

Pitcher and bowl, 3½" Christy.
#439. $14.00 – 18.00.

Snack set, Gold Christmas Tree.
#1876. $22.00 – 28.00.

Teapot, 6 cup, Gold Christmas Tree.
#1878. $80.00 – 90.00.

Tray, two-tier tidbit, Gold Christmas Tree.
#1875. $65.00 – 75.00.

Mug, 3" Holly Garland.
#2041. $18.00 – 22.00.

Cup and saucer, Holly Garland.
#1802. $25.00 – 30.00.

Plate, 9" Holly Garland.
#1804. $30.00 – 35.00.

Snack set, 8" Holly Garland.
#1402. $25.00 – 35.00.

Tray, single tidbit, Holly Garland.
#2094. $20.00 – 25.00.

Jam jar with spoon, salt and pepper, Holly with Touches of
Candy Cane Red. #035. $55.00 – 75.00 set.

Dish, three compartments, Holly Garland.
#2038. $65.00 – 75.00.

Plate, 8¼" decorated tree.
#2687. $12.00 – 15.00.

Compotes

5½" Mardi Gras.
#20438. $95.00 – 105.00.

5½"x8" Footed with fruit attached.
#2604. $95.00 – 105.00.

*5¼" White decorated with red roses and sponge gold, Only
A Rose.*
#386. $95.00 – 105.00.

7" Rose Chintz.
#650. $38.00 – 42.00.

Blue Paisley.
#2341. $18.00 – 22.00.

7½" Cosmo design.
#1083. $40.00 – 50.00.

10½" Violet design with sponge gold.
#20406. $70.00 – 80.00.

8" Latticed rim with violets and gold.
#592. $38.00 – 42.00.

7" Latticed, Wheat design.
#112. $28.00 – 32.00.

7" Paisley Fantazia.
#6805. $16.00 – 24.00.

8" Americana.
#940. $65.00 – 75.00.

Cookie Jars and Canister Sets

10" Harvest Pansy.
#7975. $45.00 – 55.00.

7¼" Americana.
#943. $125.00 – 145.00.

7½" Fruit Basket or Tutti Frutti.
#1674. $85.00 – 95.00.

6½" Pink Daisy.
#4856. $45.00 – 55.00.

Canister set, Rustic Daisy, 4 pieces.
#4115. $90.00 – 105.00.

Canister set, Hot Poppy, 4 pieces.
#5308. $100.00 – 135.00.

Canister set, Green Orchard, 4 pieces.
#3733. $95.00 – 115.00.

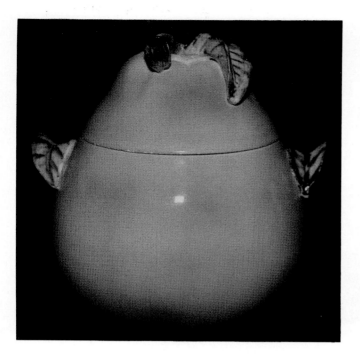

7¼" Pear with cover.
#20489. $85.00 – 95.00.

10¼" Glazed finish with adorable dog on lid.
#2482. $75.00 – 85.00.

Honey Bee.
#1279. $110.00 – 135.00.

10½" Tisket A Tasket.
#7128. $50.00 – 60.00.

10" Woodland Cookies.
#7858. $45.00 – 55.00.

7½" Dainty Miss.
#040. $150.00 – 200.00.

9½" Dutch girl.
#2366. $250.00 – 300.00.

7¼" Bluebird.
#289. $300.00 – 400.00.

Cups and Saucers

After dinner, Elegant Rose.
#634. $32.00 – 36.00.

Tea, decorated in a beautiful floral pattern.
#912. $45.00 – 55.00.

Blue with hand-painted flowers.
#801. $35.00 – 40.00.

Tea with violets, legged.
#2996. $35.00 – 40.00.

Tea, decorated in a beautiful grape pattern.
#911. $45.00 – 55.00.

Wheat design.
#20602. $18.00 – 22.00.

Rose Heirloom.
#1826. $28.00 – 32.00.

Pale background with painted flowers, pearlized inside of cup.
#2904. $20.00 – 25.00.

Cup and saucer, tea with violets.
#2300. $35.00 – 40.00.

Mug, 3¾" Rustic Daisy.
#4468. $8.00 – 12.00.

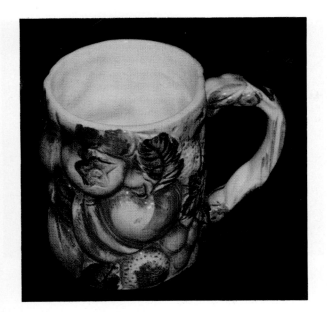

Mug, Fruits of Italy.
#1209. $11.00 – 15.00.

Mug, 4" Blue Aster.
#6496. $8.00 – 10.00.

Mustache, Fleur de Lis.
#6120. $38.00 – 42.00.

Tea, Americana.
#973. $35.00 – 40.00.

Fall of the Four Seasons
#780. $38.00 – 42.00

After dinner cup and saucer with rose design.
#124. $15.00 – 20.00.

Tea on pedestal decorated with portrait and sponge gold.
#20583. $35.00 – 40.00.

After dinner on pedestal with floral design.
#110. $28.00 – 32.00.

After dinner, Green Heritage.
#1151. $25.00 – 30.00.

Footed cup with saucer, portrait and floral design.
#20583. $35.00 – 40.00.

Brown Heritage, Floral.
#703. $20.00 – 25.00.

Mug, grape design.
#3918. $12.00 – 18.00.

Jumbo cup, Elegant Rose.
#1806. $30.00 – 35.00.

Tea, Heavenly Rose.
#2758. $38.00 – 42.00.

Tea, Happy Anniversary, Rose Chintz design.
#2425. $18.00 – 22.00.

After dinner.
#1798. $22.00 – 28.00.

Jumbo Dad.
#3400. $30.00 – 35.00.

Pine Cone design.
#2619. $15.00 – 18.00.

After dinner, gold and brown.
#253. $10.00 – 15.00.

Mug, 4¼" Washington.
#1110. $35.00 – 45.00.

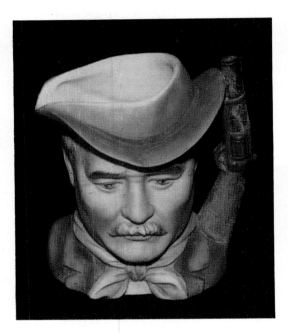

Mug, 4¼" Teddy Roosevelt.
#2191. $45.00 – 50.00.

Mug, 4¼" Lincoln.
#1113. $35.00 – 45.00.

Mug, 4¼" Robert E. Lee.
#2365. $45.00 – 55.00.

Decorative Items

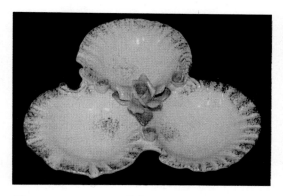

Three compartment dish with raised pink roses and sponge gold.
#1980. $50.00 – 60.00.

7", 3 compartment dish, leaf-shaped, pink with roses in relief.
#2914. $32.00 – 35.00.

6", 2 compartment dish, pink with violets.
#2332. $32.00 – 38.00.

Right: Bonbon with violets trimmed with gold. #2334. $30.00 – 35.00.

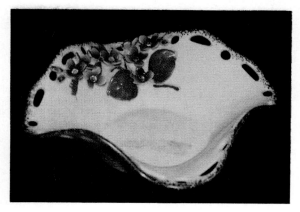

Left: 6" Latticed dish with stones and lilacs. #232. $28.00 – 32.00.

Bonbon with violets trimmed in gold.
#2334. $30.00 – 35.00.

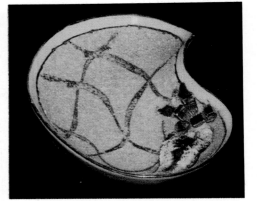

Kidney-shaped dish, Eastern Elegance.
#20567. $32.00 – 38.00.

Bonbon with violets trimmed in gold.
#2334. $32.00 – 38.00.

8½" Candy with roses on off-white with gold.
#368. $23.00 – 27.00.

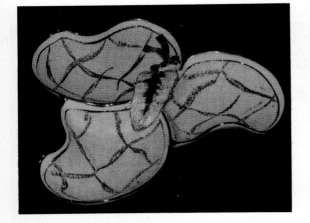

8½" 3 compartment, Eastern Elegance.
#20569. $75.00 – 85.00.

Dish with floral design and sponge gold, footed.
#8242. $65.00 – 75.00.

Leaf-shaped dish, Green Heritage.
#1860. $20.00 – 30.00.

6" Bonbon, Brown Heritage, Floral.
#20127. $28.00 – 32.00.

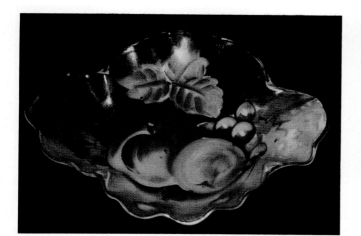

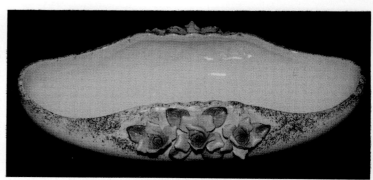

Pink porcelain with sponge gold and raised roses.
#2085. $65.00 – 85.00.

6" Bonbon, fruit design.
#20127. $28.00 – 32.00.

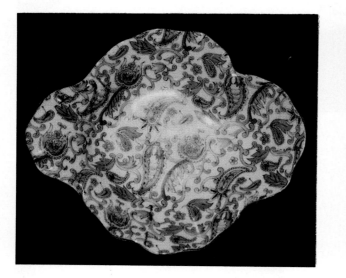

6½" Blue Paisley.
#2349. $15.00 – 20.00.

8½" Classic Elegance.
#4808. $32.00 – 38.00.

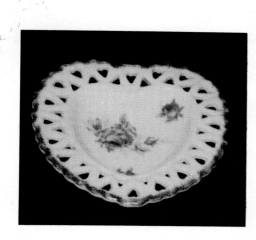

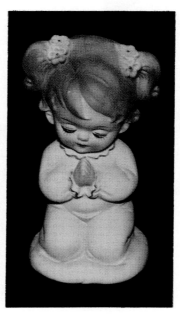

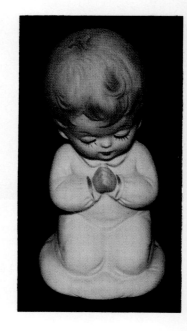

Dish, 4" latticed heart-shaped, mint
with roses or violets.
#4814. $18.00 – 22.00.

6½" Nite lite, girl in pink.
#6626. $35.00 – 45.00.

6½" Nite lite, boy in blue.
#6625. $35.00 – 45.00.

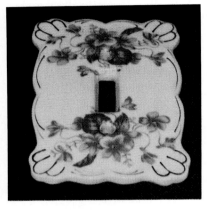

5½" x 3½" Switch plate with violets.
#197. $15.00 – 20.00.

3" Bell, pink with Forget-Me-Nots.
#8293. $25.00 – 30.00.

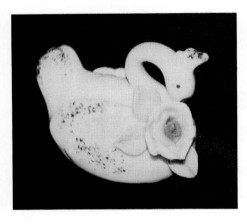

Miniature swan, glazed
china with rose trim.
#121. $28.00 – 32.00.

8" Square dish with violets.
#2874. $45.00 – 50.00.

7½" Candy dish decorated with violets.
#2560. $65.00 – 75.00.

8" Square dish with roses.
#2874. $45.00 – 50.00.

Espresso Line

#3284 – 9" Plate . . . .$18.00 – 22.00

#3283 – 7½" Plate . . . .$8.00 – 12.00

#3252 – Wisteria Cup and Saucer . . . .$12.00 – 18.00

#3251 – Sandalwood Cup and Saucer . . . .$12.00 – 18.00

#3250 – Tangerine Cup and Saucer . . . .$12.00 – 18.00

#3159 – 10¾" Wisteria Coffee Pot . . . .$85.00 – 95.00

#3163 – 4" Wisteria Sugar and Creamer . . . .$32.00 – 38.00

#3157 – 10¾" Sandalwood Coffee Pot . . . .$85.00 – 95.00

#3161 – 4" Sandalwood Sugar and Creamer . . . .$32.00 – 38.00

#3156 – 10¾" Tangerine Coffee Pot . . . .$85.00 – 95.00

#3160 – 4" Tangerine Sugar and Creamer . . . .$32.00 – 38.00

#3249 – 8" Wisteria Snack Set . . . .$15.00 – 20.00

#3248 – 8" Sandalwood Snack Set . . . .$15.00 – 20.00

#3247 – 8" Tangerine Snack Set. . . . .$15.00 – 20.00

#3408 – 4½" Wisteria A. D. Cup and Saucer . . . .$15.00 – 20.00

#3409 – 4½" Sandalwood A. D. Cup and Saucer . . . .$15.00 – 20.00

#3410 – 4½" Tangerine A. D. Cup and Saucer . . . .$15.00 – 20.00

#2990 – Tea Cup and Saucer, Yellow, Blue, Tangerine or Pumpkin . . . .$18.00 – 22.00

#3165 – 5" x 2¾" Ashtrays, Wisteria, Sandalwood, or Tangerine . . . .$5.00 – 10.00

#2991 – 4½" Ashtrays, Yellow, Tangerine, Blue, or Wisteria . . . .$3.00 – 6.00

Lefton's Espresso Line

Figurines

4½" Chinese sitting boy and girl with stone.
#127. $45.00 – 55.00 pair.

9½" Chinese man and woman with stones.
#10009. $145.00 – 165.00 pair.

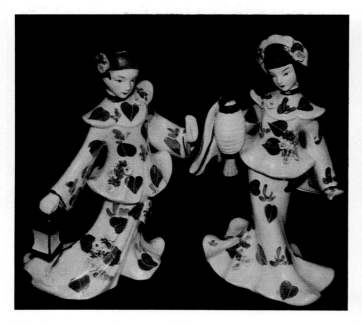

8" Chinese man and woman with lanterns, green.
#10268. $135.00 – 165.00 pair.

6½" Chinese man and woman.
#129. $80.00 – 90.00 pair.

10" Dancing lady and man, white and gold.
_#767. $225.00 – 275.00._

6¼" Lady with purse.
_#10566. $130.00 – 150.00._

5¼" Girl with flowers and two pink poodles.
_#692. $38.00 – 42.00._

6¼" Girl with hat and stole.
_#461. $70.00 – 80.00._

7½" Gay Nineties in pink.
#1573. $145.00 – 165.00.

6¼" Lady with umbrella and man with hat in hand,
white and gold.
#460. $130.00 – 140.00.

5" Lady with open umbrella.
#8696. $120.00 – 150.00.

6" Colonial lady and man, pastel bisque.
#458. $95.00 – 125.00 pair.

6" Girl with umbrella and purse.
#1571. $130.00 – 150.00.

10" Spanish dancers white, black, and gold.
#10292. $170.00 – 200.00 pair.

7½" Victorian lady with umbrella.
#585. $165.00 – 215.00.

12" Colonial woman.
#877. $155.00 – 185.00.

8" Lady, matte finish.
#612. $75.00 – 95.00.

7¼" French lady in dark bluegreen dress with
roses, holding purse.
#10229. $95.00 – 125.00.

7½" Suzette, deep color porcelain.
#5744. $135.00 – 165.00.

7" Colonial lady, bisque, Mildred.
#3046. $80.00 – 90.00.

10½" Colonial man and woman.
#2256. $350.00 – 400.00 pair.

10" Colonial man and woman.
#1705. $325.00 – 375.00 pair.

12" Provincial man and woman, carrying baskets of flowers.
#4141. $400.00 – 450.00 pair.

7" Provincial man and woman carrying flowers.
#7223. $80.00 – 100.00 pair.

10" Colonial man or woman,
Old Masters series.
#3660. $125.00 – 150.00 each.

8" Man and woman holding grapes.
#5895. $250.00 – 350.00 pair.

5¾" Ballerina.
#444. $80.00 – 95.00 set of three.

6" Red Boy, Old Masters series.
#3988. $60.00 – 70.00.

8½" Provincial boy and girl with dogs.
#5642. $225.00 – 275.00.

5½" Boy and girl in overalls.
#5667. $70.00 – 80.00 pair.

6" Tom Sawyer, bisque.
#845. $45.00 – 65.00.

6" Beck Thatcher, bisque.
#844. $45.00 – 65.00.

5¾" x 6½" There Was An Old Woman.
#1103. $120.00 – 180.00.

8" Pinkie and Blue Boy, bisque.
#387. $130.00 – 180.00 pair.

6¼" Peter, Peter, Pumpkin Eater.
#1247. $75.00 – 100.00.

4½" Pussy Cat, Pussy Cat.
#1474. $55.00 – 75.00.

8¾" Calypso dancers.
#169. $160.00 – 190.00 pair.

8¼" Surgeon.
#6819. $32.00 – 36.00.

8½" Nurse.
#6152. $40.00 – 50.00.

8¼" Stockbroker.
#7451. $55.00 – 65.00.

11" Napoleon on horse.
#4908. $285.00 – 315.00.

8" Don Quixote and Sancho Panza.
#4721. $95.00 – 110.00.

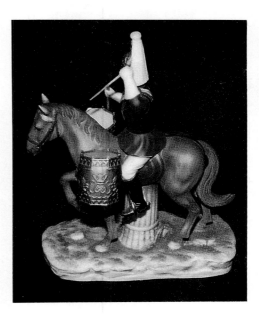

11" Drummer on horse.
#4989. $175.00 – 225.00.

4" Girl with ponytail and miniature
identical doll.
#8948. $48.00 – 52.00.

4½" Boy and girl.
#1178. $25.00 – 30.00 pair.

6½" Siamese dancers.
#493. $100.00 – 130.00.

6¼" Man with walking stick.
#2349. $40.00 – 45.00.

8" Rock-A-Bye Baby.
#1104. $150.00 – 200.00.

4" Nurse.
#8950. $32.00 – 42.00.

4" Flower girl, white with sponge gold.
#10531. $45.00 – 65.00.

Waitress, bloomer girl.
#10532. $75.00 – 95.00.

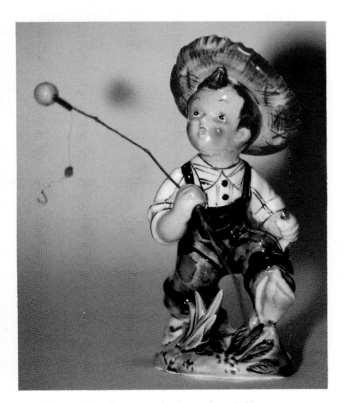

6¼" Lady with hat and flower basket, blue.
#1859. $50.00 – 60.00.

Huckleberry Finn in natural colors, glazed china.
#1009. $75.00 – 85.00.

3½" Pixie, pearl luster.
#3254. $20.00 – 25.00.

4" Pixie on mushroom watching frog.
#1191. $11.00 – 13.00.

4" Girl with poodle.
#1206. $25.00 – 30.00.

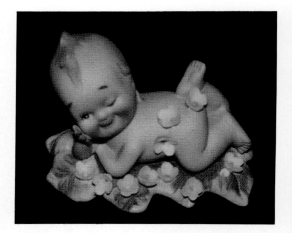

Kewpie lying on leaves with white flower petals under
and over (one broken).
#2992. $28.00 – 32.00.

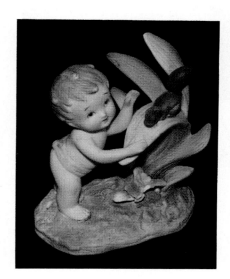

3½" Baby with squirrel.
#3056. $18.00 – 20.00.

4¾" Hi Diddle Diddle.
#1257. $100.00 – 135.00.

4½" Bloomer girl.
#843. $40.00 – 50.00.

7½" Lady, porcelain, Fifi.
#5742. $120.00 – 150.00.

7½" Boy and girl, bisque, Old Masters series.
#3990. $65.00 – 85.00 pair.

4½" Little Boy Blue.
#1249. $65.00 – 85.00.

6" Lady in Rose Chintz dress.
#851. $55.00 – 75.00.

6¼" Girl, bisque.
#133. $60.00 – 75.00 each.

7" Dancing boy and girl, bisque.
#4140. $75.00 – 95.00 pair.

7¼" Lady with lace.
#3205. $75.00 – 95.00.

7¾" Lady with shawl.
#1888. $70.00 – 80.00.

5½" Colonial boy and girl.
#3428. $26.00 – 32.00 pair.

6" French lady, dubonnet with stones.
#10337. $65.00 – 75.00.

7" Soldiers.
#181. $50.00 – 70.00 each.

4½" Boys bowling.
#005. $60.00 – 90.00 set of three.

6½" Girl, matte.
#3083. $45.00 – 55.00 each.

Wedding couple on sofa.
#4645. 3-piece set, $25.00 – 45.00.

Little Adorables.
#326. $125.00 – 145.00 set.

5¼" Colonial boy and girl, shelf sitters.
#1568. $30.00 – 40.00 pair.

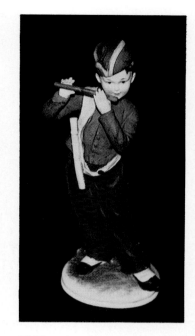

8" Piper boy, bisque.
#858. $65.00 – 75.00.

5" Kneeling boy and girl with prayerful hands.
#945. $110.00 – 130.00 pair.

5½" This Little Pig Went to Market.
#1252. $75.00 – 95.00.

5½" Little Miss Muffet.
#1106. $55.00 – 65.00.

6" Patty Cake, Patty Cake.
#1248. $55.00 – 65.00.

5¾" Humpty Dumpty.
#1250. $65.00 – 85.00.

7¼" Old Mother Hubbard.
#1105. $100.00 – 125.00.

Gingham Line

#3265 – 8 Cup coffee pot	$75.00 – 95.00
#3266 – Sugar and creamer	$35.00 – 40.00
#3267 – Tea cup and saucer	$15.00 – 20.00
#3268 – 9¼" plate	$15.00 – 20.00
#3302 – Jam jar with spoon	$30.00 – 35.00
#3297 – 8¾" Snack set	$22.00 – 28.00
#3298 – 3" Mug	$10.00 – 12.00
#3300 – 3⅝ Egg cup	$10.00 – 15.00
#3333 – 7" Cookie jar	$65.00 – 75.00
#3299 – Oil and vinegar, pair	$24.00 – 34.00
#3301 – Butter dish with cover	$15.00 – 20.00
#3336 – Salt and pepper	$12.00 – 18.00
#3273 – 8 Cup coffee pot	$75.00 – 95.00
#3274 – Sugar and creamer	$35.00 – 40.00
#3275 – Tea cup and saucer	$15.00 – 20.00
#3276 – 9¼" Plate	$15.00 – 20.00
#3314 – Jam jar with spoon	$30.00 – 35.00
#3309 – 8¾" Snack set	$22.00 – 28.00
#3310 – 3" Mug	$10.00 – 12.00
#3312 – 3⅝" Egg cup	$10.00 – 15.00
#3335 – 7" Cookie jar	$65.00 – 75.00
#3311 – Oil and vinegar, pair	$24.00 – 34.00
#3313 – Butter dish with cover	$15.00 – 20.00
#3338 – Salt and pepper	$12.00 – 18.00
#3269 – 8 Cup coffee pot	$75.00 – 95.00
#3270 – Sugar and creamer	$35.00 – 40.00
#3271 – Tea cup and saucer	$15.00 – 20.00
#3272 – 9¼" Plate	$15.00 – 20.00
#3308 – Jam jar with spoon	$30.00 – 35.00
#3303 – 8¾" Snack set	$22.00 – 28.00
#3304 – 3" Mug	$10.00 – 12.00
#3306 – 3⅝" Egg cup	$10.00 – 15.00
#3334 – 7" Cookie jar	$65.00 – 75.00
#3305 – Oil and vinegar, pair	$24.00 – 34.00
#3307 – Butter dish with cover	$15.00 – 20.00
#3337 – Salt and pepper	$12.00 – 18.00

Lefton's Gingham Line

4¾" Jam jar with spoon, Fruit Basket or Tutti Frutti.
#1680. $32.00 – 38.00.

5¾" Tea jar in white with painted vines and teacup.
#1742. $15.00 – 20.00.

4" Jam jar with spoon, Rustic Daisy.
#3858. $18.00 – 22.00.

Jam jar, with spoon, Americana.
#956. $55.00 – 85.00.

Jam jar, pear with tray and spoon.
#2844. $32.00 – 38.00.

Jam jar with plastic spoon and tray, Festival.
#2617. $32.00 – 36.00.

Jam jar with tray, Pear 'N Apple.
#4255. $22.00 – 28.00.

4½" Syrup, Sweetie.
#1333. $35.00 – 40.00.

Jam jar, Thumbelina, spoon and underplate.
#1697. $50.00 – 60.00.

5¾" Ketchup jar.
#1484. $100.00 – 125.00.

5" Instant coffee with spoon.
#744. $18.00 – 22.00.

5½" Jam jar with strawberries.
#2661. $18.00 – 22.00.

Jam jar with tray and spoon, Honey Bee.
#1280. $35.00 – 40.00.

5¼" with spoon and tray, Cabbage Cutie.
#2128. $40.00 – 45.00.

4½", Green Heritage.
#1152. $35.00 – 45.00.

Jam jar, Lilac Chintz.
#202. $35.00 – 40.00.

Cheese dish with cover, Honey Bee.
#1285. $50.00 – 60.00.

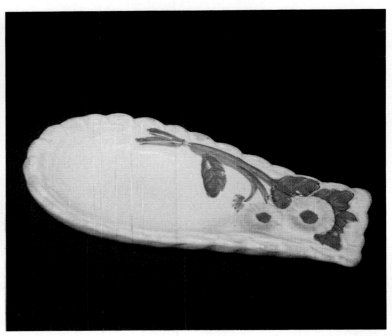

7½" Spoon rest, Rustic Daisy.
#4123. $12.00 – 15.00.

7¾" Butter dish with cover, Rustic Daisy.
#4466. $18.00 – 22.00.

6" Napkin holder, Rustic Daisy.
#5403. $17.00 – 19.00.

4¼" Bunny napkin holder with chicken salt and pepper.
#7141. $20.00 – 25.00 set.

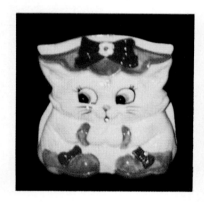

5" Napkin holder, kitten.
#1452. $15.00 – 20.00.

Condiment set, Pansies.
#3529. $40.00 – 50.00.

Condiment set, Rose Heirloom.
#1915. $65.00 – 85.00.

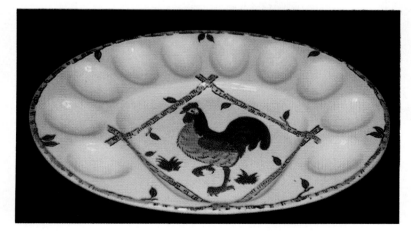

12½" Egg tray, Country Squire.
#1601. $32.00 – 38.00.

Teabag holder, Blue Paisley.
_#2354. $15.00 – 20.00._

4¾" Teabag holder, floral design.
_#8282. $5.00 – 10.00._

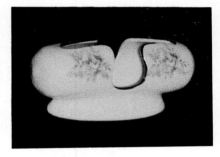

Teabag holder, flower-shaped.
#2516. $15.00 – 20.00 each.

4¼" Toothpick holder, Petite Fleurs.
_#6436. $20.00 – 25.00._

2¼" Toothpick holder, legged.
_#427. $15.00 – 20.00._

3" Egg cup, Golden Wheat.
_#20121. $15.00 – 20.00._

Butter dish with cover, Dancing Leaves.
#7309. $24.00 – 28.00.

5½" Cheese dish with cover, Miss Priss.
#1505. $200.00 – 225.00.

9" Two compartment dish, Miss Priss.
#1507. $95.00 – 125.00.

8¼" Pitcher, Bossie the Cow.
#6516. $30.00 – 35.00.

7¾" Butter dish with cover, Bossie the Cow.
#6514. $22.00 – 28.00.

Child's set, bowl and mug, Miss Priss.
#3553. $90.00 – 110.00 set.

7" Matchbox holder, Rustic Daisy.
#5402. $20.00 – 25.00.

3" Coaster, fruit design.
#20128. $9.00 – 12.00.

12" Dish, Symphony in Fruit.
#1016. $30.00 – 35.00.

9½" Casserole, Americana.
#978. $115.00 – 145.00.

15¼" Three compartment dish, Americana.
#972. $75.00 – 85.00.

6" Bone dish, Moss Rose.
#706. $10.00 – 15.00.

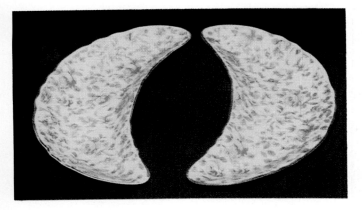

Bone dish, Blue Paisley.
#2347. $10.00 – 15.00.

11¼" x 6" Relish tray, Rustic Daisy.
#4121. $18.00 – 22.00.

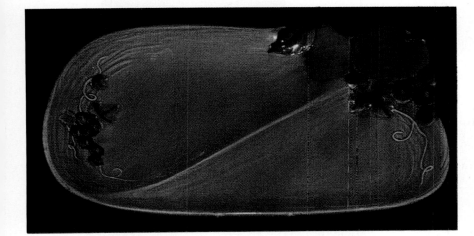

12" Two compartment, Pear 'N Apple.
#4129. $24.00 – 28.00.

13" x 7" Two compartment, Rustic Daisy.
#4122. $38.00 – 42.00.

Pitchers and Bowls

5½" Floral design with gold.
#323. $40.00 – 45.00.

6¼" Rustic Daisy.
#4126. $23.00 – 26.00.

6" Rustic Daisy.
#5565. $24.00 – 28.00.

5¼" Daisytime.
#3406. $22.00 – 28.00.

4½" White with violet design and gold.
#2565. $25.00 – 35.00.

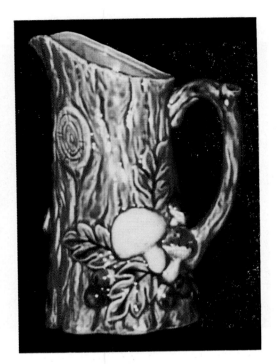

6¾" Mushroom Forest.
#6466. $19.00 – 21.00.

8½" Monk Decanter with six mugs.
#991. $55.00 – 65.00.

6¼" Green Heritage.
#4579. $55.00 – 75.00.

Brown Heritage, Floral.
#1873. $52.00 – 58.00.

3" Floral.
#4672. $20.00 – 25.00.

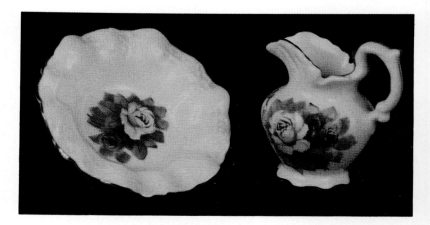

3½" Floral Bouquet.
#7254. $12.00 – 17.00.

4¼" Green Daisy.
#5777. $15.00 – 20.00.

5¼" 50th Anniversary.
#5991. $27.00 – 32.00.

Tumbleup, Green Heritage.
#1266. $100.00 – 125.00.

Planters

4338

4339

3866

4337

#4338 – *9" Lady Planter, two shapes, 3 colors.* $50.00 – 60.00

#4339 – *8" Lady Planter, three colors.* . . . .$50.00 – 60.00

#3866 – *8" Lady Planter with hat, 3 colors* . . .$30.00 – 40.00

#4337 – *7½" Lady Planter, two shapes, 3 colors* .$30.00 – 40.00

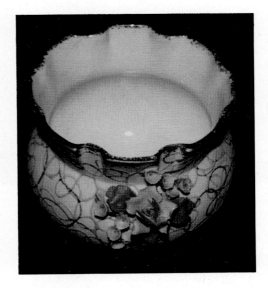

4¾" 3-legged bucket, Mardi Gras.
_#50441. $40.00 – 45.00._

5¾" Girl.
_#50265. $40.00 – 45.00._

Fan-shaped flower holder, white china with roses.
_#282. $95.00 – 105.00._

4½" Bucket, Only A Rose.
_#414. $45.00 – 50.00._

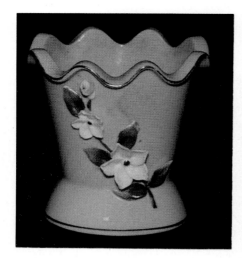

4" Pink with white flowers.
#553. $15.00 – 20.00.

6" Horse and colt.
#2171. $25.00 – 30.00.

Cowboy with sponge gold and applied flowers.
#5575. $27.00 – 35.00.

5½" Girl pushing cart, pink.
#50584. $32.00 – 38.00.

5½" Calico donkey.
#5897. $35.00 – 45.00.

7½" White luster with elf on spout, applied flowers.
#50479. $35.00 – 40.00.

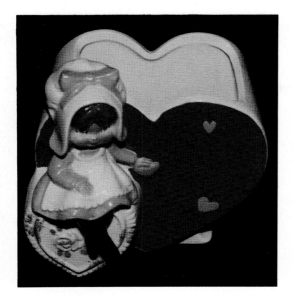

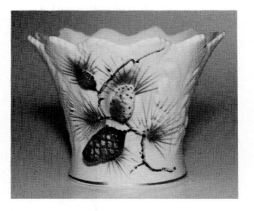

3¾" with pine cone.
#3002. $28.00 – 32.00.

4½" Heart-shaped with little girl on front, Valentine.
#6747. $15.00 – 20.00.

10¼" Fish.
#709. $22.00 – 24.00.

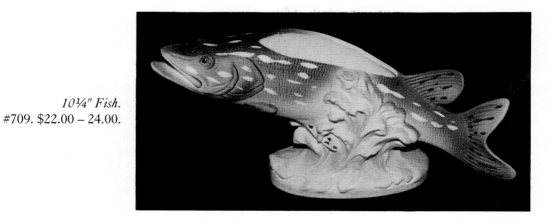

7" Ruffed grouse, matte finish.
#580. $25.00 – 30.00.

4½" Red robin.
#763. $36.00 – 43.00.

4¼" Boy and girl.
#269. $35.00 – 40.00.

4½" White luster planter with girl posed on side, applied flowers.
#2703. $15.00 – 18.00.

7" Adorable white kitten with polka dot tie.
#5741. $15.00 – 20.00.

5" Swan, Floral Bisque Bouquet.
#3782. $18.00 – 22.00.

8" Dog.
#1571. $17.00 – 21.00.

4" "Our Irish Colleen", opening 4"x4"x4".
#8202. $12.00 – 15.00.

6" Girl, glazed finish.
#4304. $20.00 – 30.00.

Pink with flowers and stones, with 2 handles in gold.
#70260. $45.00 – 50.00.

6" Train.
#6397. $20.00 – 25.00.

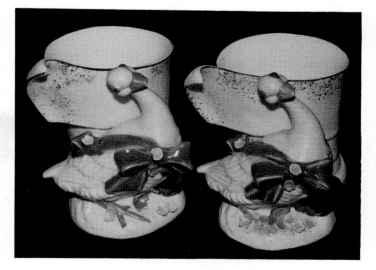

Pink ducks with sponge gold.
#5575. $27.00 – 35.00 each.

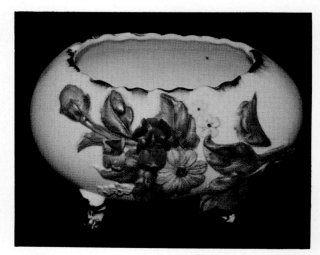

5" Egg, floral bisque.
#7171. $35.00 – 45.00.

6½" Peacock, matte.
#892. $32.00 – 38.00.

4"x4½" with 2 hearts with cupid.
#2995. $17.00 – 21.00.

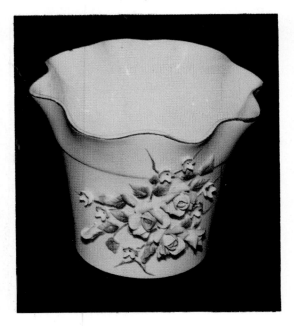

4" White bisque, with flowers.
#827. $25.00 – 30.00.

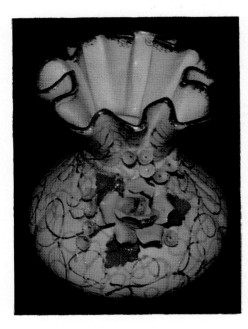

6½" Bag-shaped, Mardi Gras.
#50440. $55.00 – 65.00.

6¾" Girl.
#6094. $28.00 – 32.00.

*4½" White with painted flowers,
opening 3¾"x4"x4".*
#1171. $10.00 – 15.00.

4¾" Valentine.
#2773. $30.00 – 35.00.

6½" Pheasant in matte.
#888. $28.00 – 32.00.

8½" Lady, Collette.
#2978. $40.00 – 50.00.

6½" Lady.
#423. $45.00 – 65.00.

*4" Broken egg with rabbit girl on side
and sponge gold.*
#5815. $25.00 – 30.00.

5" Small girl with hat flower holder.
#1232. $20.00 – 25.00.

Fishing hat.
#1713. $22.00 – 32.00.

12" Sacred Heart of Jesus planter.
#3940. $28.00 – 32.00

5¼"x8½" Sprinkler with flowers and stones.
#249. $28.00 – 32.00.

5½" Modern shape, white with pink
flower.
#554. $18.00 – 22.00.

4½" Bird.
#1099. $18.00 – 22.00.

7" Fuzzy dog with cart.
#1629. $30.00 – 40.00.

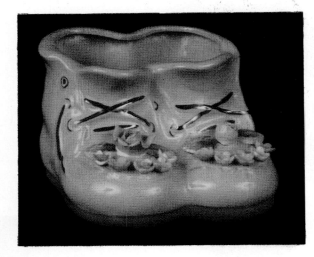

4½" Baby shoe with flowers.
#928. $15.00 – 18.00.

6½" Dutch girl.
#3318. $30.00 – 35.00.

5"x4½" Dutch shoes with boy and girl.
#5260. $60.00 – 70.00.

8" Car.
#4020. $25.00 – 35.00.

Plates

10½" Americana.
#976. $28.00 – 32.00.

8" Wheat design.
#20230. $22.00 – 24.00.

9" Brown Heritage, Floral.
#2222. $35.00 – 40.00.

9" Violets.
#2910. $30.00 – 35.00.

10" Rose Heirloom.
#1821. $30.00 – 35.00.

7½" Rose Chintz.
#658. $20.00 – 23.00.

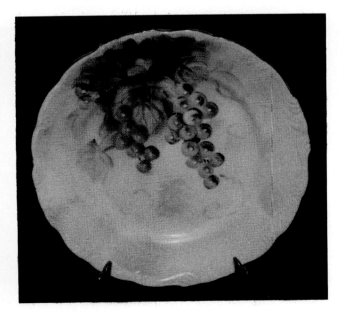

7" Festival.
#2620. $16.00 – 18.00.

8" Eastern Star design.
#105. $12.00 – 15.00.

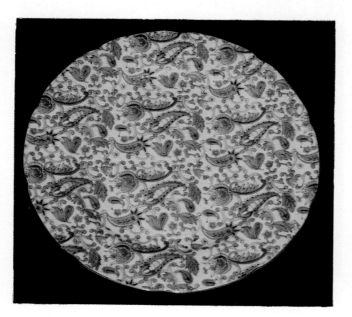

9¼" Blue Paisley.
#2337. $20.00 – 25.00.

7¼" Brown Heritage, Fruit.
#562. $28.00 – 32.00.

10" Hors d'oeuvre plate, Elegant Rose.
#2992. $45.00 – 50.00.

Reticulated around edge with painted fruit.
#711. $35.00 – 40.00.

9¼" To A Wild Rose.
#2578. $28.00 – 32.00.

10¼" Cake plate, 25th Anniversary.
#1130. $12.00 – 15.00.

9¼" Plate with plastic handle, Americana.
#939. $50.00 – 60.00.

9" Plate with plastic handle, Brown Heritage, Floral.
#185. $50.00 – 60.00.

Salt and Pepper Shakers

3" To A Wild Rose.
#2639. $18.00 – 22.00.

6¾" Rustic Daisy.
#4124. $20.00 – 25.00.

3" Honey Bee.
#1288. $22.00 – 28.00.

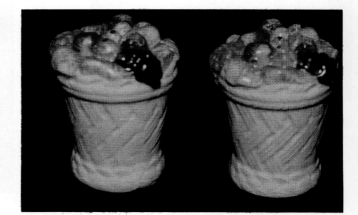

2¾" Fruit Basket.
#1657. $22.00 – 28.00.

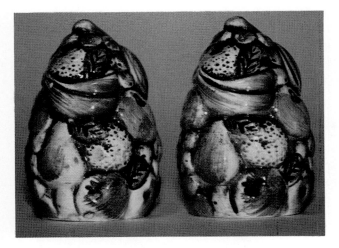

Fruits of Italy.
#1207. $12.00 – 15.00.

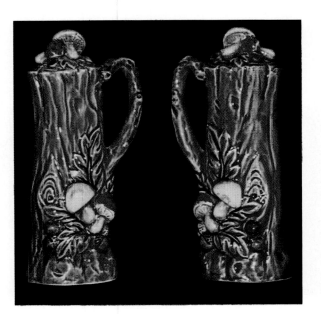

6½" Mushroom Forest.
#6355. $17.00 – 21.00.

6" Fiesta.
#5281. $20.00 – 25.00.

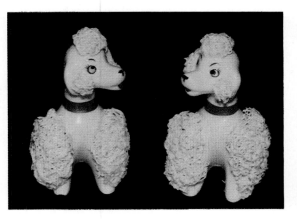

Pink poodles.
#104. $32.00 – 38.00.

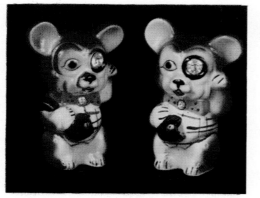

Mice with stones for eyes.
#30404. $18.00 – 22.00.

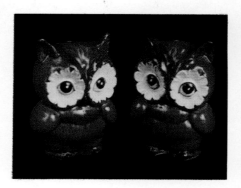

Owls.
#6836. $8.00 – 10.00.

3" Dutch boy and girl in wooden shoes.
#3207. $15.00 – 20.00.

Kitten with flowers on head.
#GZL. $25.00 – 30.00.

3½" Bossie the Cow.
#6510. $15.00 – 25.00.

Smoking Items

Cigarette set, box with two ashtrays, Lily of the Valley.
#242. $55.00 – 65.00.

Cigarette set, box with two ashtrays, Heavenly Rose.
#103. $50.00 – 55.00.

Cigarette set, 5" box, white, glazed, pink
rose trim.
#4150. $40.00 – 45.00.

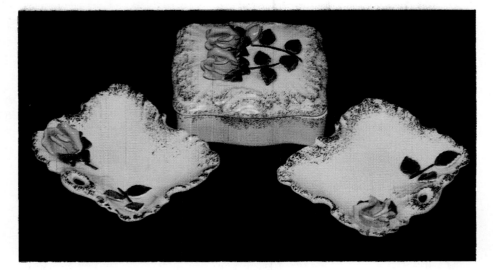

5" Hand, decorated with rose.
#717. $55.00 – 65.00.

Cigarette set, box with two ashtrays, roses and sponge gold.
#209. $50.00 – 60.00.

7" Ashtray, with roses.
#132. $28.00 – 32.00.

Ashtray, violets in leaf shape, stacked.
#934. $45.00 – 50.00.

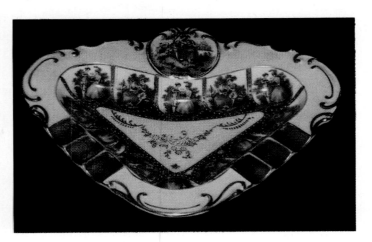

7½" Ashtray, Pink Romance with gold.
#4963. $40.00 – 45.00.

5¼" Ashtray, leaf-shaped holder attached to tray.
#1005. $18.00 – 22.00.

3½" Ashtray, with Forget-Me-Not flowers.
#4080. $25.00 – 35.00.

3½" Cigarette urn, Lily of the Valley.
#987. $35.00 – 40.00.

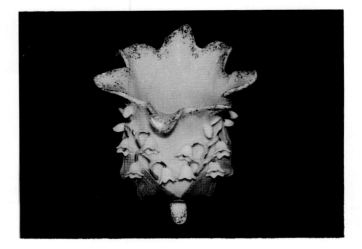

Cigarette set, holder with two ashtrays, violets.
#4557. $60.00 – 75.00.

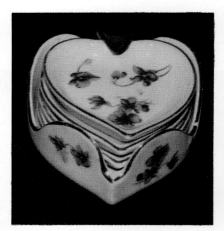

3" Ashtray, nested heart-shaped trays with holder, violets.
#4995. $25.00 – 30.00.

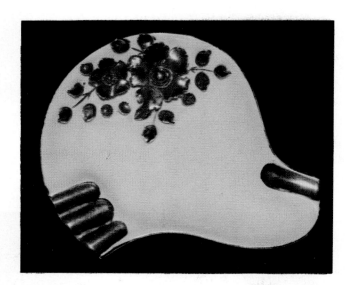

7" Ashtray, modern shape in pink with gold flowers.
#40422. $40.00 – 45.00.

3" Cigarette lighter, Gold Wheat.
#40111. $32.00 – 38.00.

3½" Ashtray with lilacs and stones touched with sponge gold.
#136. $15.00 – 18.00.

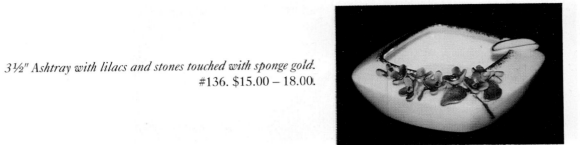

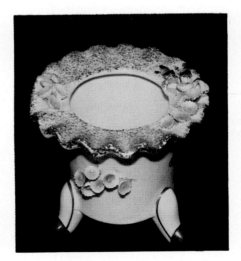

Ashtray, hand with roses and sponge gold.
#40452. $55.00 – 65.00.

Ashtrays.
#1576. $50.00 – 60.00 set of three.

Cigarette holder with Forget-Me-Not flowers.
#3600. $30.00 – 40.00.

4½" Ashtray, swan, dark green with gold roses.
#954. $35.00 – 45.00.

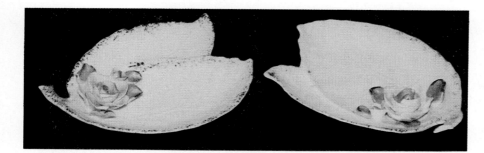

Ashtray, small leaf.
#301. $15.00 – 18.00.

4" Ashtray, Masonic with emblem.
#4345. $20.00 – 25.00.

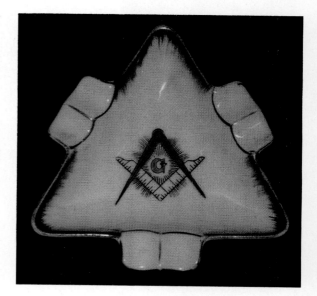

6¾" Ashtray, Eastern Star design.
#559. $20.00 – 25.00.

Cigarette set, footed holder with two ashtrays, Rose Chintz.
#654. $25.00 – 35.00.

Four nested ashtrays in holder, Golden Wheat design.
#40124. $15.00 – 18.00.

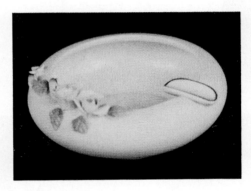

3½" Ashtray, pink bisque with flowers, inside glazed.
#1782. $10.00 – 12.00.

6" Ashtray, round with gold applied flowers.
#40424. $25.00 – 35.00.

Cigarette holder, white with blue grapes.
#2458. $10.00 – 12.00.

Snack Sets

Violets with gold.
#20054. $28.00 – 32.00.

Shell-shaped Elegant Rose.
#2124. $30.00 – 35.00.

Shell-shaped with violet design.
#2124. $30.00 – 35.00.

8¼" Moss Rose.
#3171. $18.00 – 22.00.

Magnolia.
#2599. $25.00 – 30.00.

9" Rose Heirloom.
#1074. $28.00 – 32.00.

Summertime.
#261. $28.00 – 32.00.

Americana.
#957. $30.00 – 35.00.

White, Pear 'N Apple.
#4263. $13.00 – 18.00.

8" To A Wild Rose.
#2580. $22.00 – 28.00.

Sugars and Creamers

Elegant Rose.
#2276. $65.00 – 75.00.

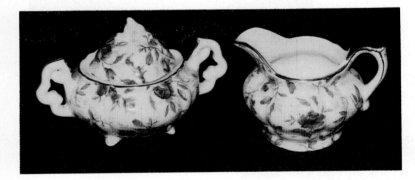

Small Rose Chintz.
#794. $30.00 – 35.00.

Violet Chintz.
#663. $35.00 – 40.00.

Cosmos.
#1078. $55.00 – 65.00.

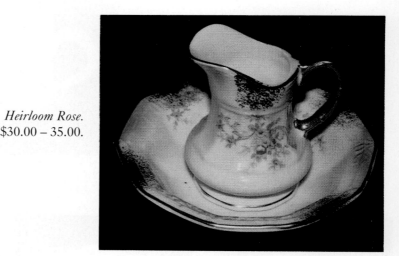

Heirloom Rose.
#1937. $30.00 – 35.00.

Gold Wheat.
#20595. $28.00 – 38.00.

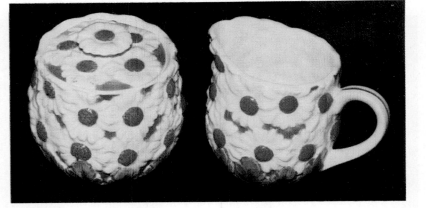

Daisytime.
#3359. $28.00 – 32.00.

Americana.
#953. $55.00 – 65.00.

Rustic Daisy.
#3856. $28.00 – 32.00.

4" Sweet Lil'.
#1425. $38.00 – 42.00.

5½ Dutch girl, sugar and creamer.
#2698. $70.00 – 85.00.

Roosters.
#2460. $45.00 – 55.00.

Heavenly Rose.
#2689. $55.00 – 65.00.

Green Heritage.
#511. $75.00 – 85.00.

Violet.
#2584. $75.00 – 85.00.

To A Wild Rose.
#2563. $40.00 – 50.00.

Fleur de Lis.
#1800. $34.00 – 38.00.

Honey Bee.
#1291. $55.00 – 65.00.

Pine Cone.
#355. $25.00 – 30.00.

Teapots and Coffee Pots

5" Teapot, 4 cup, Elegant Rose.
#2323. $110.00 – 135.00.

Teapot, Elegant Rose.
#2275. $130.00 – 180.00.

Combination teapot, sugar and creamer in violets with stippled gold.
#885. $150.00 – 195.00.

Coffee pot, Cosmos.
#1077. $110.00 – 125.00.

Teapot, Magnolia.
#2519. $175.00 – 195.00.

Teapot, Eastern Star insignia.
#2725. $60.00 – 70.00.

Teapot, decorated with pinecones.
#353. $45.00 – 55.00.

Teapot, musical Bluebird.
#734. $225.00 – 275.00.

Teapot, Americana.
#952. $135.00 – 185.00.

Teapot, Miss Priss.
#1516. $145.00 – 195.00.

Teapot, 25th Anniversary.
#279. $45.00 – 55.00.

Teapot, Blue Paisley.
#2373. $150.00 – 175.00.

Teapot, 8½" Green Heritage.
#510. $175.00 – 225.00.

Teapot, 8¼" Silver Wheat.
#2156. $60.00 – 70.00.

Coffee pot, Heavenly Rose.
#2690. $165.00 – 195.00.

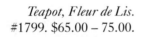

Teapot, Fleur de Lis.
#1799. $65.00 – 75.00.

Teapot, violets in Dresden shape.
#2439. $215.00 – 265.00.

Teapot, violets with gold.
#20610. $65.00 – 85.00.

Teapot, violet design.
#092. $65.00 – 85.00.

Teapot, 6 cup, Cabbage Cutie.
#2123. $85.00 – 100.00.

Teapot, 1½ cup, Rose Chintz.
#3185. $50.00 – 60.00.

Tidbit Trays

2 tier, Americana.
#942. $90.00 – 100.00

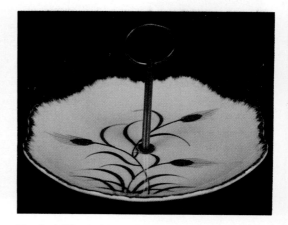

6", 3 compartment tidbit with metal handle, Elegant Rose.
#2351. $30.00 – 35.00.

Tidbit with metal handle, Rose Chintz.
#651. $30.00 – 35.00.

Single tidbit, Golden Wheat.
#20231. $20.00 – 25.00.

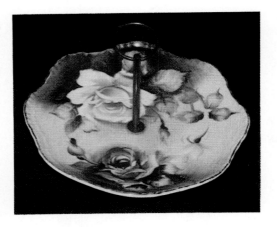

Tidbit, Brown Heritage, Floral.
#20131. $28.00 – 32.00.

2 tier tidbit, Brown Heritage, Floral.
#20129. $120.00 – 150.00.

6", 3 compartment tidbit with metal handle, violets.
#2351. $30.00 – 35.00.

2 tier tidbit, Fruit Fantasia.
#6729. $50.00 – 60.00.

Vases

7" Pitcher-shaped with colonial boy and girl.
#156. $35.00 – 40.00 pair.

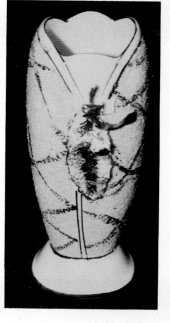

7¼" Vase with white feather,
Eastern Elegance.
#007. $35.00 – 45.00.

Pink ewer with gold flowers.
#70425. $38.00 – 42.00.

5¾" Cornucopia with lilacs and stones.
#158. $60.00 – 65.00.

6" White milk china with roses.
#833. $48.00 – 52.00.

10" Pitcher-shaped, white bisque with hand applied flowers.
#1772. $50.00 – 60.00.

6", Only A Rose.
#421. $55.00 – 65.00.

5½", Only A Rose.
#382. $75.00 – 85.00.

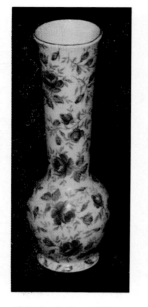

6" Pink china with Forget-Me-Not decoration, stippled gold on sand effect border.
#7294. $75.00 – 85.00.

6¼" Bud, Rose Chintz.
#679. $25.00 – 30.00.

6" Pink porcelain, Forget-Me-Not decoration.
#270. $50.00 – 60.00.

6" Pink with Forget-Me-Nots
and stones.
#70459. $50.00 – 60.00.

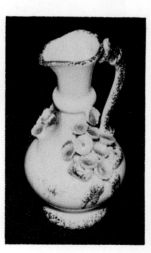

3½" Miniature with Forget-
Me-Nots and stippled gold.
#9860. $28.00 – 32.00.

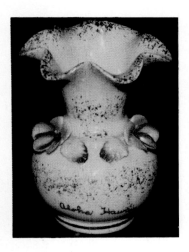

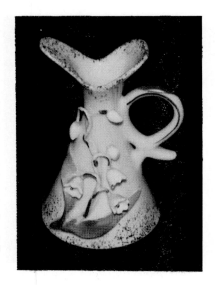

3½" with Forget-Me-Nots and stones.
#70457. $32.00 – 36.00.

2¾" Miniature, stippled gold and flowers.
#124. $30.00 – 35.00.

3¼" with Lily of the Valley.
#198. $33.00 – 38.00.

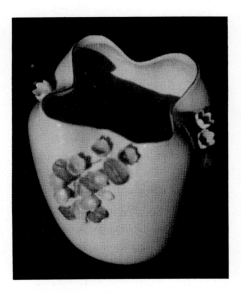

4" with hand applied flowers.
#70058. $35.00 – 40.00.

7" Ice pink bisque with applied flowers.
#1185. $60.00 – 65.00.

*6½" Bud vase, ice pink bisque with
applied flowers.
#1184. $48.00 – 52.00.*

*6" Pink bisque with applied flowers.
#1036. $60.00 – 65.00.*

*6¼" White bisque with grapes, 2
handles.
#2181. $32.00 – 36.00.*

*6" Fluted, milk china with roses.
#839. $45.00 – 55.00.*

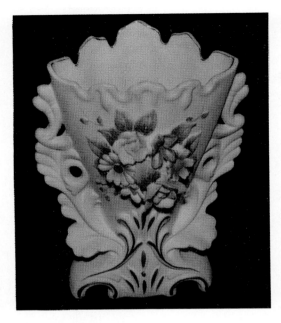

6½" Floral Bisque Bouquet.
#7217. $32.00 – 38.00.

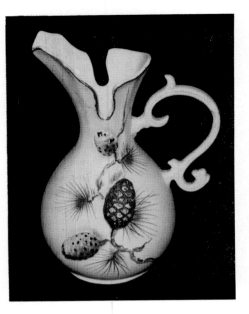

6" Ewer with pinecones.
#2461. $30.00 – 35.00.

5" Glazed head vase, Scarlett.
#051. $95.00 – 115.00.

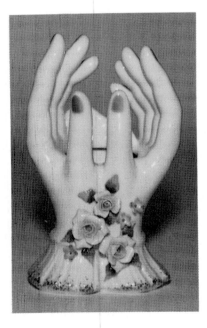

5" Hands in white glaze with hand
applied flowers.
#893. $45.00 – 55.00.

4" Beige Italian Romance.
#781. $20.00 – 25.00.

5¾" Luscious Lilac.
#2948. $30.00 – 35.00.

7" Flower in white bisque, Flower Garland.
#2447. $28.00 – 32.00.

6¼" Pink with flowers.
#191. $17.00 – 21.00.

6" Pitcher, Woodrose line.
#267. $30.00 – 35.00.

7½" Pitcher-shaped with flowers in
pink bisque.
#1031. $35.00 – 45.00.

6¾" Bud, pink with flowers and
stones.
#70541. $35.00 – 45.00.

6¼" Brown bisque with
cherubs.
#1597. $9.00 – 12.00.

5½" Hands, white bisque with flowers.
#1787. $45.00 – 55.00.

*7½" Pink china decorated in gold
with yellow rose.*
#906. $75.00 – 85.00.

7¾" Macaw.
#1544. $80.00 – 90.00.

7½ " Crane.
#1546. $80.00 – 90.00.

Wall Plaques and Wall Pockets

4" Comical lady or man.
#4249. $12.00 – 15.00 each.

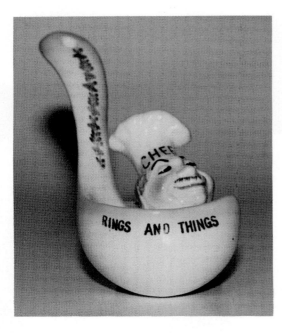

RINGS AND THINGS

8" Rings and things.
#535. $40.00 – 50.00.

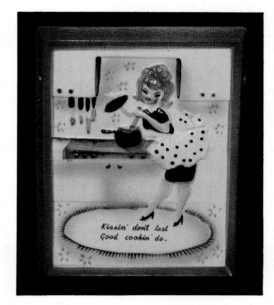

8" Kissin' Don't Last.
#3124. $17.00 – 21.00.

5" Dainty Miss.
#6767. $95.00 – 125.00.

Pitcher and bowl, Rustic Daisy.
#4467. $30.00 – 40.00 pair.

8" Ladies' hat, Rustic Daisy.
#4360. $20.00 – 25.00.

Colonial lady and man in pastel green and pink.
#3438. $95.00 – 110.00.

8¼" Boy and girl.
#4769. $60.00 – 65.00 pair.

8½" Boy and girl in ornate frame.
#350. $60.00 – 70.00 pair.

Oval frame with boy and girl in bisque.
#5826. $100.00 – 150.00 pair.

Colonial man and woman holding baskets of flowers.
#1753. $130.00 – 160.00 pair.

8¼" Oval, colonial boy and girl.
#6967. $50.00 – 55.00 pair.

7"x7¼" Heart shape, latticed, decorated with fruit.
#522. $15.00 – 18.00.

8" Latticed plate decorated with fruit design.
#60588. $24.00 – 28.00.

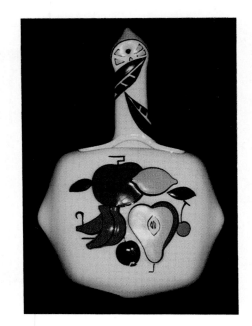

Scallop shape plate with fruit design on dark background.
#6994. $25.00 – 30.00.

9¼" Frying pan with fruit design.
#2112. $18.00 – 22.00.

5" Round plaque, black with red rose.
#331. $28.00 – 32.00 each.

3½" Baby on leaf in porcelain.
#8145. $28.00 – 32.00.

4½" Wall pocket decorated with fruit.
#6839. $35.00 – 45.00.

4½"x4", Three dimensional with child's
head in relief, fuzzy hair.
#984. $32.00 – 38.00.

7" Violin with rose and sponge
gold.
#369. $28.00 – 32.00.

3" Angel in bisque with gold.
#2342. $10.00 – 12.00.

7" Wall pocket, boy with basket.
#2628. $75.00 – 95.00.

7½" Violin in glazed ceramic
with raised pansy.
#105. $28.00 – 32.00.

8" Round plate with ship design, hand painted.
#6718. $22.00 – 27.00.

7" Latticed, flower design with hair line gold.
#2509. $15.00 – 18.00.

5" Dog's head.
#7437. $12.00 – 15.00.

6" Round with hand applied flowers in matte finish.
#668. $12.00 – 15.00.

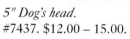

6½" Round with pinecones.
#2478. $15.00 – 18.00.

8½" Rectangular shape with fruit in
relief. #4691. $8.00 – 11.00.

8" Latticed with red cardinal.
#622. $18.00 – 22.00.

5¼" with flowers in matte.
#1176. $28.00 – 32.00.

8" Lord's Prayer, Elegant Rose.
#6347. $24.00 – 34.00.

8" Fruit design.
#6927. $25.00 – 35.00.

8" Round with Fruit design.
#60408. $21.00 – 27.00.

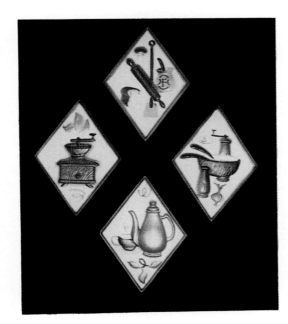

Group of kitchen utensils.
#3003. $28.00 – 32.00 4-piece set.

COLLECTOR BOOKS

Informing Today's Collector

For over two decades we have been keeping collectors informed on trends and values in all fields of antiques and collectibles.

DOLLS, FIGURES & TEDDY BEARS

4707	A Decade of **Barbie** Dolls & Collectibles, 1981–1991, Summers	$19.95
4631	**Barbie** Doll Boom, 1986–1995, Augustyniak	$18.95
2079	**Barbie** Doll Fashion, Volume I, Eames	$24.95
4846	**Barbie** Doll Fashion, Volume II, Eames	$24.95
3957	**Barbie** Exclusives, Rana	$18.95
4632	**Barbie** Exclusives, Book II, Rana	$18.95
4557	**Barbie**, The First 30 Years, Deutsch	$24.95
4847	**Barbie** Years, 1959–1995, 2nd Ed., Olds	$17.95
3310	**Black Dolls**, 1820–1991, Perkins	$17.95
3873	**Black Dolls**, Book II, Perkins	$17.95
3810	**Chatty Cathy Dolls**, Lewis	$15.95
1529	Collector's Encyclopedia of **Barbie** Dolls, DeWein	$19.95
4882	Collector's Encyclopedia of **Barbie** Doll Exclusives and More, Augustyniak	$19.95
2211	Collector's Encyclopedia of **Madame Alexander Dolls**, Smith	$24.95
4863	Collector's Encyclopedia of **Vogue Dolls**, Izen/Stover	$29.95
3967	Collector's Guide to **Trolls**, Peterson	$19.95
4571	**Liddle Kiddles**, Identification & Value Guide, Langford	$18.95
3826	Story of **Barbie**, Westenhouser	$19.95
1513	**Teddy Bears & Steiff** Animals, Mandel	$9.95
1817	**Teddy Bears & Steiff** Animals, 2nd Series, Mandel	$19.95
2084	**Teddy Bears, Annalee's & Steiff** Animals, 3rd Series, Mandel	$19.95
1808	Wonder of **Barbie**, Manos	$9.95
1430	World of **Barbie** Dolls, Manos	$9.95
4880	World of **Raggedy Ann** Collectibles, Avery	$24.95

TOYS, MARBLES & CHRISTMAS COLLECTIBLES

3427	**Advertising Character** Collectibles, Dotz	$17.95
2333	Antique & Collector's **Marbles**, 3rd Ed., Grist	$9.95
3827	Antique & Collector's **Toys**, 1870–1950, Longest	$24.95
3956	Baby Boomer **Games**, Identification & Value Guide, Polizzi	$24.95
4934	**Breyer Animal** Collector's Guide, Identification and Values, Browell	$19.95
3717	**Christmas** Collectibles, 2nd Edition, Whitmyer	$24.95
4976	**Christmas** Ornaments, Lights & Decorations, Johnson	$24.95
4737	**Christmas** Ornaments, Lights & Decorations, Vol. II, Johnson	$24.95
4739	**Christmas** Ornaments, Lights & Decorations, Vol. III, Johnson	$24.95
4649	Classic Plastic **Model Kits**, Polizzi	$24.95
4559	Collectible **Action Figures**, 2nd Ed., Manos	$17.95
3874	Collectible Coca-Cola Toy **Trucks**, deCourtivron	$24.95
2338	Collector's Encyclopedia of **Disneyana**, Longest, Stern	$24.95
4958	Collector's Guide to **Battery Toys**, Hultzman	$19.95
4639	Collector's Guide to **Diecast Toys & Scale Models**, Johnson	$19.95
4651	Collector's Guide to **Tinker Toys**, Strange	$18.95
4566	Collector's Guide to **Tootsietoys**, 2nd Ed., Richter	$19.95
4720	The Golden Age of **Automotive Toys**, 1925–1941, Hutchison/Johnson	$24.95
3436	Grist's Big Book of **Marbles**	$19.95
3970	Grist's Machine-Made & Contemporary **Marbles**, 2nd Ed.	$9.95
4723	**Matchbox** Toys, 1947 to 1996, 2nd Ed., Johnson	$18.95
4871	**McDonald's Collectibles**, Henriques/DuVall	$19.95
1540	**Modern Toys** 1930–1980, Baker	$19.95
3888	**Motorcycle** Toys, Antique & Contemporary, Gentry/Downs	$18.95
4953	Schroeder's Collectible **Toys**, Antique to Modern Price Guide, 4th Ed.	$17.95
1886	Stern's Guide to **Disney** Collectibles	$14.95
2139	Stern's Guide to **Disney** Collectibles, 2nd Series	$14.95
3975	Stern's Guide to **Disney** Collectibles, 3rd Series	$18.95
2028	**Toys**, Antique & Collectible, Longest	$14.95
3979	**Zany Characters** of the Ad World, Lamphier	$16.95

FURNITURE

1457	American **Oak** Furniture, McNerney	$9.95
3716	American **Oak** Furniture, Book II, McNerney	$12.95
1118	Antique **Oak** Furniture, Hill	$7.95
2271	Collector's Encyclopedia of **American** Furniture, Vol. II, Swedberg	$24.95
3720	Collector's Encyclopedia of **American** Furniture, Vol. III, Swedberg	$24.95
3878	Collector's Guide to **Oak** Furniture, George	$12.95
1755	Furniture of the **Depression Era**, Swedberg	$19.95
3906	**Heywood-Wakefield** Modern Furniture, Rouland	$18.95

1885	**Victorian** Furniture, Our American Heritage, McNerney	$9.95
3829	**Victorian** Furniture, Our American Heritage, Book II, McNerney	$9.95

JEWELRY, HATPINS, WATCHES & PURSES

1712	Antique & Collector's **Thimbles** & Accessories, Mathis	$19.95
1748	Antique **Purses**, Revised Second Ed., Holiner	$19.95
1278	Art Nouveau & Art Deco **Jewelry**, Baker	$9.95
4850	Collectible **Costume Jewelry**, Simonds	$24.95
3875	Collecting Antique **Stickpins**, Kerins	$16.95
3722	Collector's Ency. of **Compacts, Carryalls & Face Powder Boxes**, Mueller	$24.95
4854	Collector's Ency. of **Compacts, Carryalls & Face Powder Boxes**, Vol. II	$24.95
4940	**Costume Jewelry**, A Practical Handbook & Value Guide, Rezazadeh	$24.95
1716	Fifty Years of Collectible **Fashion Jewelry**, 1925–1975, Baker	$19.95
1424	**Hatpins** & Hatpin Holders, Baker	$9.95
4570	Ladies' **Compacts**, Gerson	$24.95
1181	100 Years of Collectible **Jewelry**, 1850–1950, Baker	$9.95
4729	**Sewing Tools** & Trinkets, Thompson	$24.95
2348	20th Century Fashionable Plastic **Jewelry**, Baker	$19.95
4878	Vintage & Contemporary **Purse Accessories**, Gerson	$24.95
3830	Vintage **Vanity Bags & Purses**, Gerson	$24.95

INDIANS, GUNS, KNIVES, TOOLS, PRIMITIVES

1868	Antique **Tools**, Our American Heritage, McNerney	$9.95
1426	**Arrowheads** & Projectile Points, Hothem	$7.95
4943	Field Guide to **Flint Arrowheads & Knives** of the North American Indian	$9.95
2279	**Indian Artifacts** of the Midwest, Hothem	$14.95
3885	**Indian Artifacts** of the Midwest, Book II, Hothem	$16.95
4870	**Indian Artifacts** of the Midwest, Book III, Hothem	$18.95
1964	**Indian Axes** & Related Stone Artifacts, Hothem	$14.95
2023	**Keen Kutter** Collectibles, Heuring	$14.95
4724	Modern **Guns**, Identification & Values, 11th Ed., Quertermous	$12.95
2164	**Primitives**, Our American Heritage, McNerney	$9.95
1759	**Primitives**, Our American Heritage, 2nd Series, McNerney	$14.95
4730	Standard **Knife** Collector's Guide, 3rd Ed., Ritchie & Stewart	$12.95

PAPER COLLECTIBLES & BOOKS

4633	**Big Little Books**, Jacobs	$18.95
4710	Collector's Guide to **Children's Books**, Jones	$18.95
1441	Collector's Guide to **Post Cards**, Wood	$9.95
2081	Guide to Collecting **Cookbooks**, Allen	$14.95
2080	Price Guide to **Cookbooks** & Recipe Leaflets, Dickinson	$9.95
3973	**Sheet Music** Reference & Price Guide, 2nd Ed., Pafik & Guiheen	$19.95
4654	**Victorian Trade Cards**, Historical Reference & Value Guide, Cheadle	$19.95
4733	**Whitman Juvenile Books**, Brown	$17.95

GLASSWARE

4561	Collectible **Drinking Glasses**, Chase & Kelly	$17.95
4642	Collectible **Glass Shoes**, Wheatley	$19.95
4937	Coll. **Glassware** from the 40s, 50s & 60s, 4th Ed., Florence	$19.95
1810	Collector's Encyclopedia of **American Art Glass**, Shuman	$29.95
4938	Collector's Encyclopedia of **Depression Glass**, 13th Ed., Florence	$19.95
1961	Collector's Encyclopedia of **Fry Glassware**, Fry Glass Society	$24.95
1664	Collector's Encyclopedia of **Heisey Glass**, 1925–1938, Bredehoft	$24.95
3905	Collector's Encyclopedia of **Milk Glass**, Newbound	$24.95
4936	Collector's Guide to **Candy Containers**, Dezso/Poirier	$19.95
4564	**Crackle Glass**, Weitman	$19.95
4941	**Crackle Glass**, Book II, Weitman	$19.95
2275	**Czechoslovakian Glass** and Collectibles, Barta/Rose	$16.95
4714	**Czechoslovakian Glass** and Collectibles, Book II, Barta/Rose	$16.95
4716	**Elegant Glassware** of the Depression Era, 7th Ed., Florence	$19.95
1380	Encyclopedia of **Pattern Glass**, McClain	$12.95
3981	Ever's Standard **Cut Glass** Value Guide	$12.95
4659	**Fenton** Art Glass, 1907–1939, Whitmyer	$24.95
3725	**Fostoria**, Pressed, Blown & Hand Molded Shapes, Kerr	$24.95
4719	**Fostoria**, Etched, Carved & Cut Designs, Vol. II, Kerr	$24.95
3883	**Fostoria** Stemware, The Crystal for America, Long & Seate	$24.95
4644	**Imperial Carnival Glass**, Burns	$18.95
3886	**Kitchen Glassware** of the Depression Years, 5th Ed., Florence	$19.95

4725	Pocket Guide to **Depression Glass**, 10th Ed., Florence	$9.95
5035	Standard Encyclopedia of **Carnival Glass**, 6th Ed., Edwards/Carwile	$24.95
5036	Standard **Carnival Glass** Price Guide, 11th Ed., Edwards/Carwile	$9.95
4875	Standard Encyclopedia of **Opalescent Glass**, 2nd ed., Edwards	$19.95
4731	**Stemware Identification**, Featuring Cordials with Values, Florence	$24.95
3326	**Very Rare Glassware** of the Depression Years, 3rd Series, Florence	$24.95
4732	**Very Rare Glassware** of the Depression Years, 5th Series, Florence	$24.95
4656	**Westmoreland Glass**, Wilson	$24.95

POTTERY

4927	**ABC Plates & Mugs**, Lindsay	$24.95
4929	**American Art Pottery**, Sigafoose	$24.95
4630	**American Limoges**, Limoges	$24.95
1312	**Blue & White Stoneware**, McNerney	$9.95
1958	So. Potteries **Blue Ridge Dinnerware**, 3rd Ed., Newbound	$14.95
1959	**Blue Willow**, 2nd Ed., Gaston	$14.95
4848	**Ceramic Coin Banks**, Stoddard	$19.95
4851	Collectible **Cups & Saucers**, Harran	$18.95
4709	Collectible **Kay Finch**, Biography, Identification & Values, Martinez/Frick	$18.95
1373	Collector's Encyclopedia of **American Dinnerware**, Cunningham	$24.95
4931	Collector's Encyclopedia of **Bauer Pottery**, Chipman	$24.95
3815	Collector's Encyclopedia of **Blue Ridge Dinnerware**, Newbound	$19.95
4932	Collector's Encyclopedia of **Blue Ridge Dinnerware**, Vol. II, Newbound	$24.95
4658	Collector's Encyclopedia of **Brush-McCoy Pottery**, Huxford	$24.95
2272	Collector's Encyclopedia of **California Pottery**, Chipman	$24.95
3811	Collector's Encyclopedia of **Colorado Pottery**, Carlton	$24.95
2133	Collector's Encyclopedia of **Cookie Jars**, Roerig	$24.95
3723	Collector's Encyclopedia of **Cookie Jars**, Book II, Roerig	$24.95
4939	Collector's Encyclopedia of **Cookie Jars**, Book III, Roerig	$24.95
4638	Collector's Encyclopedia of **Dakota Potteries**, Dommel	$24.95
5040	Collector's Encyclopedia of **Fiesta**, 8th Ed., Huxford	$19.95
4718	Collector's Encyclopedia of **Figural Planters & Vases**, Newbound	$19.95
3961	Collector's Encyclopedia of **Early Noritake**, Alden	$24.95
1439	Collector's Encyclopedia of **Flow Blue China**, Gaston	$19.95
3812	Collector's Encyclopedia of **Flow Blue China**, 2nd Ed., Gaston	$24.95
3813	Collector's Encyclopedia of **Hall China**, 2nd Ed., Whitmyer	$24.95
3431	Collector's Encyclopedia of **Homer Laughlin China**, Jasper	$24.95
1276	Collector's Encyclopedia of **Hull Pottery**, Roberts	$19.95
3962	Collector's Encyclopedia of **Lefton China**, DeLozier	$19.95
4855	Collector's Encyclopedia of **Lefton China**, Book II, DeLozier	$19.95
2210	Collector's Encyclopedia of **Limoges Porcelain**, 2nd Ed., Gaston	$24.95
2334	Collector's Encyclopedia of **Majolica Pottery**, Katz-Marks	$19.95
1358	Collector's Encyclopedia of **McCoy Pottery**, Huxford	$19.95
3963	Collector's Encyclopedia of **Metlox Potteries**, Gibbs Jr.	$24.95
3837	Collector's Encyclopedia of **Nippon Porcelain**, Van Patten	$24.95
2089	Collector's Ency. of **Nippon Porcelain**, 2nd Series, Van Patten	$24.95
1665	Collector's Ency. of **Nippon Porcelain**, 3rd Series, Van Patten	$24.95
4712	Collector's Ency. of **Nippon Porcelain**, 4th Series, Van Patten	$24.95
1447	Collector's Encyclopedia of **Noritake**, Van Patten	$19.95
3432	Collector's Encyclopedia of **Noritake**, 2nd Series, Van Patten	$24.95
1037	Collector's Encyclopedia of **Occupied Japan**, 1st Series, Florence	$14.95
1038	Collector's Encyclopedia of **Occupied Japan**, 2nd Series, Florence	$14.95
2088	Collector's Encyclopedia of **Occupied Japan**, 3rd Series, Florence	$14.95
2019	Collector's Encyclopedia of **Occupied Japan**, 4th Series, Florence	$14.95
2335	Collector's Encyclopedia of **Occupied Japan**, 5th Series, Florence	$14.95
4951	Collector's Encyclopedia of **Old Ivory China**, Hillman	$24.95
3964	Collector's Encyclopedia of **Pickard China**, Reed	$24.95
3877	Collector's Encyclopedia of **R.S. Prussia**, 4th Series, Gaston	$24.95
1034	Collector's Encyclopedia of **Roseville Pottery**, Huxford	$19.95
1035	Collector's Encyclopedia of **Roseville Pottery**, 2nd Ed., Huxford	$19.95
4856	Collector's Encyclopeida of **Russel Wright**, 2nd Ed., Kerr	$24.95
4713	Collector's Encyclopedia of **Salt Glaze Stoneware**, Taylor/Lowrance	$24.95
3314	Collector's Encyclopedia of **Van Briggle** Art Pottery, Sasicki	$24.95
4563	Collector's Encyclopedia of **Wall Pockets**, Newbound	$19.95
2111	Collector's Encyclopedia of **Weller Pottery**, Huxford	$29.95
3876	Collector's Guide to **Lu-Ray Pastels**, Meehan	$18.95
3814	Collector's Guide to **Made in Japan** Ceramics, White	$18.95
4646	Collector's Guide to **Made in Japan** Ceramics, Book II, White	$18.95
4565	Collector's Guide to **Rockingham**, The Enduring Ware, Brewer	$14.95
2339	Collector's Guide to **Shawnee Pottery**, Vanderbilt	$19.95
1425	**Cookie Jars**, Westfall	$9.95

3440	**Cookie Jars**, Book II, Westfall	$19.95
4924	Figural & Novelty **Salt & Pepper Shakers**, 2nd Series, Davern	$24.95
2379	Lehner's Ency. of **U.S. Marks** on Pottery, Porcelain & China	$24.95
4722	**McCoy Pottery**, Collector's Reference & Value Guide, Hanson/Nissen	$19.95
3825	**Purinton Pottery**, Morris	$24.95
4726	**Red Wing Art Pottery**, 1920s–1960s, Dollen	$19.95
1670	**Red Wing Collectibles**, DePasquale	$9.95
1440	**Red Wing Stoneware**, DePasquale	$9.95
1632	**Salt & Pepper Shakers**, Guarnaccia	$9.95
5091	**Salt & Pepper Shakers** II, Guarnaccia	$18.95
2220	**Salt & Pepper Shakers** III, Guarnaccia	$14.95
3443	**Salt & Pepper Shakers** IV, Guarnaccia	$18.95
3738	**Shawnee Pottery**, Mangus	$24.95
4629	Turn of the Century **American Dinnerware**, 1880s–1920s, Jasper	$24.95
4572	**Wall Pockets** of the Past, Perkins	$17.95
3327	**Watt Pottery** – Identification & Value Guide, Morris	$19.95

OTHER COLLECTIBLES

4704	Antique & Collectible **Buttons**, Wisniewski	$19.95
2269	Antique **Brass & Copper** Collectibles, Gaston	$16.95
1880	Antique **Iron**, McNerney	$9.95
3872	Antique **Tins**, Dodge	$24.95
4845	Antique **Typewriters & Office Collectibles**, Rehr	$19.95
1714	**Black** Collectibles, Gibbs	$19.95
1128	**Bottle** Pricing Guide, 3rd Ed., Cleveland	$7.95
4636	**Celluloid Collectibles**, Dunn	$14.95
3718	Collectible **Aluminum**, Grist	$16.95
3445	Collectible **Cats**, An Identification & Value Guide, Fyke	$18.95
4560	Collectible **Cats**, An Identification & Value Guide, Book II, Fyke	$19.95
4852	Collectible **Compact Disc** Price Guide 2, Cooper	$17.95
2018	Collector's Encyclopedia of **Granite Ware**, Greguire	$24.95
3430	Collector's Encyclopedia of **Granite Ware**, Book 2, Greguire	$24.95
4705	Collector's Guide to **Antique Radios**, 4th Ed., Bunis	$18.95
3880	Collector's Guide to **Cigarette Lighters**, Flanagan	$17.95
4637	Collector's Guide to **Cigarette Lighers**, Book II, Flanagan	$17.95
4942	Collector's Guide to **Don Winton Designs**, Ellis	$19.95
3966	Collector's Guide to **Inkwells**, Identification & Values, Badders	$18.95
4947	Collector's Guide to **Inkwells**, Book II, Badders	$19.95
4948	Collector's Guide to **Letter Openers**, Grist	$19.95
4862	Collector's Guide to **Toasters & Accessories**, Greguire	$19.95
4652	Collector's Guide to **Transistor Radios**, 2nd Ed., Bunis	$16.95
4653	Collector's Guide to **TV Memorabilia**, 1960s–1970s, Davis/Morgan	$24.95
4864	Collector's Guide to **Wallace Nutting Pictures**, Ivankovich	$18.95
1629	**Doorstops**, Identification & Values, Bertoia	$9.95
4567	Figural **Napkin Rings**, Gottschalk & Whitson	$18.95
4717	Figural **Nodders**, Includes Bobbin' Heads and Swayers, Irtz	$19.95
3968	**Fishing Lure** Collectibles, Murphy/Edmisten	$24.95
4867	**Flea Market Trader**, 11th Ed., Huxford	$9.95
4944	**Flue Covers**, Collector's Value Guide, Meckley	$12.95
4945	**G-Men and FBI Toys** and Collectibles, Whitworth	$18.95
5043	**Garage Sale & Flea Market Annual**, 6th Ed.	$19.95
3819	**General Store Collectibles**, Wilson	$24.95
4643	**Great American West** Collectibles, Wilson	$24.95
2215	Goldstein's **Coca-Cola** Collectibles	$16.95
3884	Huxford's **Collectible Advertising**, 2nd Ed.	$24.95
2216	**Kitchen Antiques**, 1790–1940, McNerney	$14.95
4950	The **Lone Ranger**, Collector's Reference & Value Guide, Felbinger	$18.95
2026	**Railroad** Collectibles, 4th Ed., Baker	$14.95
4949	**Schroeder's Antiques** Price Guide, 16th Ed., Huxford	$12.95
5007	**Silverplated Flatware**, Revised 4th Edition, Hagan	$18.95
1922	Standard **Old Bottle** Price Guide, Sellari	$14.95
4708	Summers' **Guide to Coca-Cola**	$19.95
4952	Summers' Pocket Guide to **Coca-Cola** Identifications	$9.95
3892	**Toy & Miniature Sewing Machines**, Thomas	$18.95
4876	**Toy & Miniature Sewing Machines**, Book II, Thomas	$24.95
3828	Value Guide to **Advertising Memorabilia**, Summers	$18.95
3977	Value Guide to **Gas Station** Memorabilia, Summers & Priddy	$24.95
4877	**Vintage Bar Ware**, Visakay	$24.95
4935	The **W.F. Cody Buffalo Bill** Collector's Guide with Values	$24.95
4879	**Wanted to Buy**, 6th Edition	$9.95

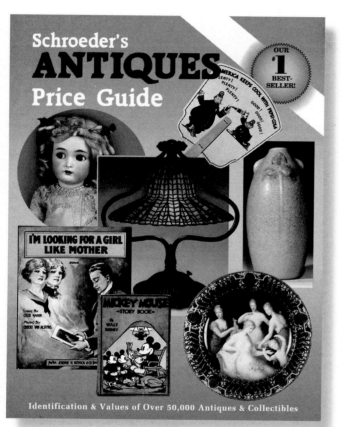